I0119489

# Strategic Rest
# *in Leadership*

## The N.A.P Framework

Erin C. Wilson, Ed.D

Kellie M. Dixon, Ed.D

STRATEGIC REST IN LEADERSHIP

ISBN: 979-8-218-51567-6

STRATEGIC REST IN LEADERSHIP

STRATEGIC REST IN LEADERSHIP

# DEDICATION

To the leaders and aspiring leaders who are shaping the future with vision and resilience: this book, *Strategic Rest in Leadership,* is dedicated to you. May it offer you the insights and tools to balance your drive with the essential practice of restorative leadership. In your quest to lead with impact, may you find strength in stillness and wisdom in reflection.

STRATEGIC REST IN LEADERSHIP

# CONTENTS

# ACKNOWLEDGMENTS

We are profoundly grateful to those who have entrusted us with the privilege of leading and have honored our commitment to integrating strategic rest into our leadership journey. Your support and willingness to embrace this balance have been both inspiring and essential.

### Dr. Dixon's Acknowledgments

In this journey of leadership, I honor those I have led, whose collaboration and trust have inspired me every step of the way. I also pay tribute to my ancestors, whose guiding spirits have illuminated the path toward the oasis of strategic rest. Their wisdom transcends titles, reminding us that true leadership is rooted in connection and compassion.

### Dr. Wilson's Acknowledgments

I want to express my deepest gratitude to my parents, Earl and Emily Chambers, for instilling the importance of rest in my life, and to my husband, Fredarick, for his unwavering support. Thank you to Dr. Erica Chambers for your invaluable feedback and reassurance. A special thanks to Dr. Whitnee Boyd, for being a true friend, sounding board, and the best retreat partner I could ask for. And to Dr. Kellie Dixon, I am forever grateful for your encouragement to put my passion into words. It is an honor to call you a dear friend, trusted business partner, and now, co-author.

# FOREWORD

In a world that values relentless hustle and non-stop productivity, it's easy for leaders to forget one of the most critical elements of sustained success: rest. This book, *Strategic Rest in Leadership*, reminds us that true leadership isn't just about powering through; it's about pacing yourself, knowing when to push forward, and when to step back and recharge.

Strategic rest is about more than taking breaks. It's about recognizing when to pause, recharge, and reflect, so you can lead from a place of strength and centeredness. As you journey through these pages, I encourage you to embrace rest not as a retreat, but as an essential part of your leadership strategy. Rest doesn't hinder success—it amplifies it.

As a holistic wellness practitioner, I've witnessed the transformative power of rest in improving well-being and performance. Leaders are not immune to burnout. In fact, they are often more vulnerable to it. The responsibilities, decisions, and pressures that come with leadership require not just intelligence and drive, but also sustainability. Rest, when woven into the fabric of leadership, becomes a catalyst for effectiveness, not a disruption to it. There is an undeniable connection between well-being and performance. Leaders who prioritize strategic rest not only cultivate resilience within themselves, but also inspire their teams to embrace a healthier, more balanced approach to work. This is not about weakness or slowing down. It's about embracing a strategy that enables leaders to be at their best—focused, creative, and equipped to make sound decisions.

The NAP (Nurture, Assess, Prioritize) Framework offers a

structured approach, while the chapters delve deeply into the why and how of integrating rest in a way that complements leadership. Whether you're a seasoned executive or a leader in the making, this book offers insights and tools that will transform how you approach your role.

As you reach the final pages of *Strategic Rest in Leadership*, I hope you've gained more than just practical strategies. I hope you've felt a shift in how you view leadership itself. Leadership is not a race—it's a marathon, one that requires pacing, reflection, and the ability to rest strategically to reach new heights of success.

This is your invitation to lead with purpose, balance, and, above all, with the wisdom that rest is not an afterthought, but a cornerstone of true leadership excellence. The path to greatness is not about doing more—it's about doing what truly matters, and sometimes, that starts with rest. Now, it's time to step forward, not with fatigue but with renewed energy and clarity. Lead well. Lead wisely. And remember—rest is your ally.

Rest Well,

*Dr. Avery Atkinson*
Holistic Wellness Practitioner
Medical Chaplain
Owner, A2G Wellness Co
www.averyatkinson.com

# STRATEGIC REST IN LEADERSHIP

# How to use this book

Welcome to *Strategic Rest in Leadership*! This book is crafted to help you integrate strategic rest into your leadership practice, enhancing your effectiveness and overall well-being. Here's a practical guide on how to use this book effectively:

## Begin with the Foundations

Start by reading **Chapter 1: Role of Rest in Effective Leadership** to understand the critical importance of rest in leadership. This chapter introduces the concept and sets the stage for why strategic rest is a game changer for effective leadership.

## Grasp the Core Concepts

Move on to **Chapter 2: Understanding Strategic Rest** to dive deeper into what strategic rest entails. This chapter will provide you with a foundational understanding of the principles and benefits of integrating rest into your leadership approach.

## Explore the NAP Framework

**Chapter 3, The NAP Framework**, offers a structured approach to strategic rest. Study this chapter to learn about the NAP (Nurture, Assess, and Prioritize) framework, which will guide you in implementing rest strategies effectively.

## Put Theory into Practice

In **Chapter 4: Strategic Rest in Action**, you'll find practical applications and strategies for incorporating strategic rest into your daily routine. This chapter includes actionable steps to help you translate theory into practice.

## Embrace the Benefits

**Chapter 5, Embracing the Power of Strategic Rest,**
discusses how to fully leverage the benefits of strategic rest.
This chapter will help you understand how embracing these
practices can lead to improved leadership outcomes and
personal well-being.

## Foster Collective Rest

**Chapter 6: Collective Strategic Rest** explores the
importance of incorporating strategic rest within teams and
organizations. Learn how to create a culture of rest and
support collective well-being among your colleagues.

## Use the Resources

Refer to the **Appendices: Resources and Tools** for
additional materials that can support your journey. This
section includes practical resources, tools, and tips to help
you apply the concepts from the book effectively.

## Reflect and Implement

As you read through the chapters, reflect on your current
practices and identify areas for improvement. Implement the
action plans and strategies discussed to integrate strategic rest
into your leadership style.

## Review and Adjust

Periodically review your progress and adjust your strategies
based on what you've learned. Leadership is an ongoing
journey, and adapting your approach to rest will help you stay
effective and balanced.

## Connect and Share

Consider discussing the book's concepts with peers, mentors, or within a group setting. Sharing insights and experiences can enhance your understanding and application of strategic rest.

By following this guide, you'll navigate *Strategic Rest in Leadership* effectively, applying its principles to become a more balanced and impactful leader. Enjoy the transformative journey towards better leadership and well-being!

Let's tap in,

Dr. Erin C. Wilson
CEO & Principal Consultant of Design Ideal Consulting
www.designidealconsulting.com

Dr. Kellie M. Dixon *(call me Dr. K)*
CEO/Founder of Clear Pathway Consulting Services LLC
www.clearpathwaycs.com

To **rest strategically in leadership** means to purposefully incorporate periods of rest and recovery into a leadership role or strategy. This involves recognizing the importance of downtime not just for personal well-being, but as a critical component of effective leadership. Strategic rest can help maintain clarity of thought, prevent burnout, and enhance decision-making and problem-solving abilities.

In essence, it means planning and managing rest periods in a way that aligns with long-term goals and overall leadership effectiveness, ensuring that leaders can remain focused, energized, and effective in their roles.

# Chapter 1
# Role of rest in effective leadership

*"Rest is wealth" - Dr. Erin Wilson*

When we think of great leaders, we often associate them with a range of inspiring qualities: visionary, decisive, innovative, supportive, collaborative. In almost any discussion about leadership, these words rise to the surface. But how often do we hear leaders praised for something as simple—and essential—as rest? The truth is, not often enough.

In many cultures, hard work and long hours are badges of honor, symbols of dedication and success. Rest, on the other hand, is sometimes misunderstood as a lack of commitment. We've romanticized the image of the tireless leader—the one who's always "on," always sacrificing personal well-being for the good of the organization. Modern society measures worth by productivity and output, often ignoring the immense value that rest can bring. But when we cut through the misconceptions about rest, we uncover a powerful truth: rest is not a weakness—it's a strength. And when used effectively, it can transform not just individual performance, but the success of entire organizations.

As a leader, prioritizing rest isn't just about personal well-being, it's about long-term effectiveness and resilience. When you intentionally take time to recharge, you create space for deeper connections, both personally and professionally. More than that, you set an example for those you lead, giving them permission to do the same. By prioritizing rest, you can shift the culture of an organization, creating an environment where well-being is valued, and where people can show up as their best selves.

In leadership, rest is a game-changer. The demands placed on leaders—making critical decisions, leading teams, driving organizational goals—are immense. Without rest, burnout is inevitable, and burnout diminishes productivity, clouds judgment, and impairs decision-making. In fact, the absence of rest can rob you of the very skills that define great leadership: creativity, problem-solving, and emotional control. Leaders who embrace rest don't just survive the pressures of leadership—they thrive. They approach challenges with renewed energy, tackle problems with creativity, and maintain the clarity needed to lead with confidence.

Perhaps most importantly, leaders who prioritize rest cultivate a higher level of emotional intelligence. Emotional intelligence—the ability to understand, connect with, and inspire others—is essential to leading effectively. It's what allows leaders to build trust, motivate teams, and navigate the complexities of interpersonal dynamics. And rest is the key to enhancing emotional intelligence. By prioritizing time to recharge, leaders develop greater self-awareness, empathy, and emotional regulation. They become better equipped to handle pressure, communicate with compassion, and make decisions that take both the big picture and the finer details into account. This, in turn, fosters a work culture rooted in positivity and support.

But rest doesn't just bolster emotional intelligence—it also fuels creativity and innovation. Many of the best ideas, the breakthrough moments, happen when we step back and give our minds space to wander. Rest is where the dots connect, where strategic visions are born. Leaders who prioritize downtime are the ones who can step away from the grind long enough to think strategically, dream big, and position their teams for long-term success.

The lesson is clear: rest isn't just a personal necessity—it's a professional strategy. Leaders who embrace rest aren't just taking care of themselves—they're unlocking new levels of creativity, enhancing emotional intelligence, and setting the stage for sustainable growth. They're showing their teams that success isn't about relentless hustle—it's about intentional recovery. Rest is the fuel that keeps the engine of leadership running, and those who master it will find themselves at the helm of organizations that are not only successful, but thriving.

# CHAPTER 2
# UNDERSTANDING STRATEGIC REST

*Emma, a brand-new vice president at a corporation, had been working tirelessly for weeks, fueled by an unrelenting determination to complete her project before the deadline. Each night, she stayed up late, her eyes straining under the harsh glow of her computer screen, and each morning she dragged herself out of bed, her body protesting with every step. Despite her best efforts, the exhaustion caught up with her, and she found herself making more mistakes and taking longer to complete tasks. One afternoon, she dozed off at her desk and missed a crucial meeting that could have provided the breakthrough she needed. If only she had taken the time to rest and recharge, she would have been sharper, more focused, and far more productive. Instead, her fatigue led to missed opportunities and a project that fell short of its potential.*

The necessity of rest for peak cognitive and physical performance is something that, ironically, many of us have overlooked for most of our lives—despite overwhelming evidence showing how vital it is. Think back to kindergarten for a moment. Can you feel the cool plastic of your nap mat beneath you, the gentle hum of the classroom as your teacher urged you to close your eyes? For some, those moments of rest came easily—like a soft escape into a world of calm. But for others, even as children, our racing minds wouldn't allow us to drift off. The fear of missing out on something—anything—was enough to keep us restless, wide awake, and unaware of the gift we were ignoring.

What if we told you that by understanding the power of strategic rest, you could finally grasp a concept that we've been struggling with since childhood? A concept that has the power to unlock your highest potential, sharpen your focus, and recharge your creativity. From that nap mat to your chair in the boardroom, the need for rest hasn't changed. What has changed is our mindset—a mindset that mistakenly equates constant motion with progress.

As children, we didn't realize it, but skipping those nap times left us crankier, more prone to meltdowns, and less able to enjoy the very playtime we were so determined not to miss. The same cycle plagues even the most accomplished adults today. We still think that by resting, we'll miss something important. But here's the truth: strategic rest is what empowers us to fully engage in what matters most. It's the key to sustained energy, emotional balance, and, most critically, high performance. As a certified Meta Performance™ Coach, I (Dr. K) encourage you to go beyond high performance and ask yourself: *What am I capable of when I rest strategically?*

When we embrace strategic rest, we're not simply recovering from fatigue—we're replenishing the wellspring of creativity, focus, and decision-making capacity. This isn't just about catching up on sleep (though that's vital, too). It's about embracing different kinds of rest that fuel every part of our being. Physical rest is necessary to recharge the body. Mental rest, through mindfulness, clears the clutter in our minds. Emotional rest, through relaxation techniques, soothes the stress that often clouds our judgment.

Leaders who master the art of strategic rest become not just more effective—they become visionary. They're able to outlast burnout, approach complex problems with clear eyes, and generate fresh solutions when others are running on empty. They make better decisions, inspire those around them, and create cultures where growth and innovation thrive. By making rest a priority, you're not just enhancing your personal performance—you're unlocking the creative potential of your entire team, leading with purpose, and positioning your organization for long-term success.

Have you experienced the fear of missing out when you rest? It's an illusion. The real magic happens when you intentionally pause, reflect, and recharge. That's when you're at your best, ready to lead with clarity, resilience, and creativity. Strategic rest is the secret ingredient to success that we all knew deep down—back when we first closed our eyes on those nap mats—but are only just now starting to appreciate as the key to unlocking our full potential.

*Wellness and Types of rest*

Have you ever found yourself stuck in an activity that you just didn't enjoy? You glance at the clock, hoping the time moves faster, your mind racing with all the other things you'd rather be doing. Meanwhile, you look over and see the person next to you—not watching the clock, not fidgeting or sighing, but actually enjoying themselves. You can't help but wonder: how could this person possibly be having fun when you're so miserable?

The truth is, fun is subjective. What energizes one person can leave another drained. It's easy to assume that everyone sees the world as we do, but people are motivated by different things. We have unique strengths, interests, and preferences. That's why an experience that feels like a chore to one person can feel like joy to someone else.

Social psychology explains this through the concept of homophily—the idea that people tend to connect with others who are like themselves. Authors McPherson, Smith-Lovin, and Cook noted similarity breeds connection. It's natural to bond over shared activities and common interests, which often helps create a sense of camaraderie. However, as our social circles expand and we're exposed to a wider range of experiences, it becomes clear that the concept of 'fun' isn't one-size-fits-all. It's highly subjective, shaped by cultural backgrounds, personal experiences, and individual personality traits.

---

*Rest is my sanctuary, a time when deadlines and obligations simply melt away, leaving me in a space of pure tranquility. It's when I can let go of decision-making and truly be in the moment, whether that's for ten minutes or two weeks. For me, rest means being grounded in the here and now, with my thoughts centered on where I am rather than scattered across a million distractions. It's not just about pausing what I'm doing—it's about embracing a state of being where I'm fully connected to myself and the present moment. Rest is my chance to reconnect, recharge, and savor the simple beauty of just being. - Dr. K*

---

Similarly, rest is a complex and multi-faceted process. It's more than just physical regeneration, it's about attending to every dimension of our well-being. Wellness is not a single idea but a collection of dimensions that touch every part of life: physical, emotional, social, spiritual, intellectual, environmental, and occupational well-being. These areas cannot thrive on effort alone. They also need restoration.

Dr. Saundra Dalton-Smith's framework on the **7 Types of Rest** shows us that rest is more than sleep. It comes in seven forms: physical, mental, emotional, social, sensory, spiritual, and creative. Each type of rest supports a different dimension. Physical rest strengthens the body. Mental and creative rest refresh the mind. Emotional and social rest restore relationships. Sensory rest brings calm. Spiritual rest anchors us in meaning. This view of rest has reshaped how we approach wellness. It is not about working harder in each area, but about giving ourselves the right kind of rest to stay whole.

Emotional wellness, for example, involves maintaining positive emotions, managing stress, and building resilience. Environmental wellness, on the other hand, is about creating a peaceful space free of clutter and noise—an environment that allows you to recharge. Financial well-being, often overlooked in conversations about rest, is about achieving stability and peace of mind through responsible money management. When our finances are in order, we can rest easier, knowing we have security. Intellectual well-being involves resting the mind in ways that foster learning, creativity, and problem-solving. By giving our minds the chance to slow down and focus, we become more open to new ideas and better equipped to tackle challenges.

Occupational wellness, which speaks directly to work-life balance, is about setting boundaries and creating space for activities that bring us joy outside of the workplace. This isn't just about punching the clock and going home. It's about engaging in activities that make life meaningful, allowing you to return to work more energized and focused. Physical wellness is perhaps the most recognized form of rest, involving sleep, nutrition, exercise, and practices that allow the body to recover. But social wellness, which emphasizes the importance of deep connections and the sense of belonging we derive from our relationships, is just as critical.

Human connection is restorative, and spending time with people who lift you up is a powerful form of rest.

Finally, spiritual wellness addresses something even deeper—a sense of purpose and connection to something greater than yourself. This might come from religious practice, meditation, or simply aligning your life with your personal values. When we nurture our spiritual selves, we cultivate inner peace and clarity, which helps us lead with purpose and authenticity.

By acknowledging and nurturing these diverse forms of rest, we can achieve holistic wellness. This not only enhances our overall quality of life, but it also enables us to lead more effectively. Whether in our personal or professional lives, understanding rest as a multi-dimensional process allows us to recharge in ways that support our growth and resilience, making us better equipped to face challenges and seize opportunities with clarity and strength.

*The impact of rest on decision-making and creativity*

Rest isn't just about catching more sleep—it's about deliberately nurturing both your mind and body in ways that fuel effective leadership. True rest gives leaders the focus and clarity they need to fully assess situations, balance competing perspectives, and make decisions that align with long-term strategic goals. When leaders are well-rested, they think clearly, evaluate risks with precision, and make decisions that drive both personal and organizational success. But when rest is neglected, judgment falters, impulsivity creeps in, and even the sharpest minds can make hasty choices that miss the mark.

Beyond sleep, rest is about creating space for activities that renew your mental energy and spark creativity. Whether it's engaging in leisure activities, practicing meditation, or simply reflecting, these moments of downtime are critical for giving your mind the chance to reset. These mental pauses are when ideas begin to connect, memories are organized, and information is processed. This is how leaders discover patterns, embrace new perspectives, and uncover innovative solutions to challenges. By prioritizing rest in all its forms, you unlock the ability to approach problems with fresh insights and creative energy.

Strategic rest plays a pivotal role in helping leaders build resilience against mental fatigue—a hidden but powerful enemy of creativity and sound decision-making. Continuous mental exertion without enough breaks leads to exhaustion, dulling the brain's ability to innovate and analyze complex situations. But by intentionally scheduling breaks and taking mental pauses throughout the day, leaders can refresh their focus and sustain high levels of cognitive performance. This proactive rest strategy fuels a mindset of resilience, embracing continuous learning and creative adaptation to whatever challenges arise.

Rest is also deeply connected to emotional regulation, a key ingredient in both creative thinking and wise decision-making. By engaging in activities that promote relaxation—whether through fun hobbies or stress-relief techniques—leaders can reduce stress hormones and lift their mood. Leaders who prioritize emotional rest are more equipped to manage their feelings, communicate clearly, and create a collaborative environment where creativity thrives. When leaders take rest seriously, they unlock their full potential, inspiring innovation, cultivating smart decision-making, and driving sustainable success in today's fast-paced, competitive world.

*Aligning Motivation with Strategic Rest*

Let's talk about motivations and how they shape the way we lead and live. Enter Core Strengths®, a powerful tool we use to explore the SDI 2.0 methodology, originally introduced by Elias Porter in 1971. This framework identifies three core motives that drive our behaviors: Nurturant (motivated by people), Directive (motivated by performance), and Autonomous (motivated by process). These motivations explain why we think, feel, and act in certain ways, and they significantly influence our effectiveness, well-being, and overall success.

*But here's the key*: when you integrate strategic rest into your life, you can better align your actions with these core motives, allowing you to thrive, not just survive.

For those with a Nurturant motive—who are driven by a desire to support others and maintain harmony—strategic rest is a game-changer. When things are going smoothly, Nurturant individuals find energy in uplifting and helping others. But during conflict, they often focus on restoring balance, sometimes through compromise or accommodation. This can be emotionally draining. By embracing strategic rest, Nurturant individuals can recharge and sustain their ability to support others effectively. They come back with renewed empathy and energy, ready to collaborate and lead with a full heart.

For Directive individuals, whose motivation is rooted in achieving results and excelling, rest is equally essential. These leaders thrive on setting goals and overcoming challenges, often asserting themselves when conflict arises. Strategic rest gives Directive individuals the chance to recalibrate. It offers them the clarity and mental space to tackle obstacles with fresh energy and sharp focus, ensuring they stay at the top of their game without burning out.

And then there are the Autonomous individuals, who value logical order and independence. They seek self-reliance and prefer to chart their own path. For them, strategic rest provides an opportunity to reflect and refocus, enabling them to align their actions with their internal motivations and core strengths.

By understanding these core motives and integrating purposeful rest, individuals can manage their energy more effectively, align their actions with what truly drives them, and ultimately experience greater fulfillment—both personally and professionally. The real magic happens when you combine strategic rest with an awareness of your core strengths. It's the key to unlocking your full potential and deepening your connections with others, setting the stage for meaningful success.

As you begin to embrace the power of strategic rest, you'll find a valuable tool in our **Strategic Rest Readiness Assessment** located in **Appendix A**. This assessment is designed to help you gauge how well you've integrated rest into your leadership style and pinpoint areas for improvement. Aligned with the **NAP framework** (discussed in the next chapter), this resource will offer you insights into your current rest habits, ensuring that the way you approach rest fuels both your personal well-being and your professional impact.

STRATEGIC REST IN LEADERSHIP

# CHAPTER 3
# THE NAP FRAMEWORK

In any leadership role—whether in a corporate boardroom, running your own business, or guiding community initiatives—the demands are immense, and the pressures are constant. To thrive in this environment, it's crucial to have more than just grit and perseverance. You need a holistic approach to both leadership development and personal well-being. By now, you've likely grasped the importance of strategic rest, but understanding it is just the beginning. The real challenge lies in consistently integrating it into your leadership routine in a way that enhances both your performance and well-being.

As coaches and consultants, we've worked with countless leaders who once believed that rest was a luxury they couldn't afford. They held tightly to the belief that endless hustle was the only path to success—that if they just pushed a little harder, sacrificed a little more, they'd reach that elusive finish line. Yet, they often found that leadership isn't a sprint—it's a marathon that requires endurance that's only sustainable with strategic, purposeful rest.

After guiding these leaders to reframe their relationship with rest, we saw firsthand how this simple but profound shift unlocked new levels of creativity, achievement, and resilience. Inspired by these transformations, we set out to develop a tool that would help more leaders incorporate rest as a strategic asset. This led to the creation and the development of the NAP Framework (Figure 1).

The NAP Framework is designed to boost leadership effectiveness by focusing on three core pillars: **Nurture, Assess, and Prioritize**.

Figure 1. The N.A.P Framework

The first pillar, **Nurture**, centers on self-care, professional development, and building strong support networks. To truly lead others, you must first nurture yourself. This includes the basics—getting enough sleep, eating well, and exercising regularly—as these are foundational to your physical and mental resilience. But nurturing goes beyond just the basics. It's about continually feeding your professional growth. Lifelong learning, whether through seminars, workshops, or personal development retreats, keeps you sharp, adaptable, and open to new ideas that can transform your leadership style.

Equally important is nurturing your relationships. Building robust support systems (more on this when we discuss Collective Strategic Rest) within and outside your organization ensures you have the guidance, feedback, and camaraderie necessary to navigate the complex challenges of leadership. Leaders don't succeed alone, and by fostering these networks, you create an environment where you can thrive.

The second pillar, **Assess**, is all about turning the focus inward and checking in with yourself. It's easy to get swept up in the day-to-day grind, but real growth and well-being come from regularly reflecting on your own mental, emotional, and physical health. Are you feeling burned out? Are there stressors you've been ignoring?

By taking the time to assess where you're at, you give yourself the chance to course-correct before things spiral. This is your opportunity to pause, breathe, and ask the important questions: How am I really doing? What do I need more of in my life? What can I let go of? Regular self-assessment helps you recognize when you're out of balance and allows you to make intentional adjustments so you can show up as your best self, fully aligned and energized for whatever comes next.

The third pillar, **Prioritize**, is all about getting intentional with your time and energy. Rest and well-being don't just happen—they require the same focus and commitment as any other goal in your life. It's time to put your needs at the top of the list, just like you would with your most important tasks.

Start by setting SMART goals (Specific, Measurable, Achievable, Relevant, and Time-bound) to create a roadmap for incorporating rest into your daily routine. What does rest look like for you? Maybe it's setting aside time for a walk, practicing mindfulness, renting a posh hotel room to getaway for a day or two (*Dr. Wilson's favorite*), playing video games and hitting the gym for a workout (*Dr. K's favorites*), or ensuring you get to bed at a certain time each night. Make these goals clear, measurable, and achievable so you can track your progress and see how prioritizing rest impacts your life positively.

Next, take it a step further by incorporating HARD goals (Heartfelt, Animated, Required, and Difficult), as defined by Mark Murphy. These goals bring passion and purpose into the mix. They connect deeply to what truly matters to you—whether it's improving your health, fostering better relationships, or pursuing a passion that energizes you. HARD goals push you to commit fully and inspire you to keep moving forward, even when it's challenging.

Once you've set your goals, make sure you're allocating the right resources to achieve them. That means investing in what supports your well-being—whether it's taking time for self-care, engaging in activities that recharge you, or seeking guidance when you need it. It's about intentionally creating space in your life for what restores you.

When you prioritize rest and well-being alongside your goals, you're not just improving your performance—you're creating a sustainable lifestyle that allows you to thrive. By integrating the principles of **Nurture, Assess, and Prioritize**, you're building a framework that strengthens your resilience, helps you stay focused on what truly matters, and ensures you show up as your best self every day.

This is how you achieve long-term success—not just in your professional life, but in your personal well-being too.

Now, let's dive deeper into each component of the framework, exploring how these pillars work together to foster a leadership style that's both high-performing and sustainable.

*Nurture*

**Nurture** is where it all begins. Self-care is often seen as a luxury—something we squeeze in when everything else is done. But let's flip that script. Self-care isn't selfish, it's foundational. It's the cornerstone of your well-being, and without it, everything else crumbles. You can't lead on empty. So, let's ask the real question: Are you giving yourself the care you need to thrive?

That means setting routines that prioritize your well-being—whether it's getting enough sleep, staying active, or eating in a way that fuels your body and mind. If you haven't made these a priority, consider this your wake-up call. Start now. These aren't just small habits, they're the foundation for building mental resilience—a superpower that lets you handle stress, stay sharp, and perform at your highest level. And here's the thing: when you model self-care as a leader, you give your team and the people around you permission to do the same. You set the standard that self-care is not only okay—it's essential to being an effective leader.

But nurturing yourself doesn't stop at physical health. Professional development is another vital piece of the puzzle. Lifelong learning isn't just a buzzword—it's how you stay ahead, adapt, and continue to grow as a leader. This means actively seeking out opportunities that sharpen your skills, whether it's attending seminars, workshops, or taking part in leadership retreats. These aren't just events—they're moments of transformation, where you gain the tools, insights, and strategies that fuel your leadership journey.

Over the years, we've seen firsthand how leadership can feel isolating. No matter how high you climb, leadership often means carrying the weight of tough decisions, navigating uncharted waters, and sometimes feeling like you're going at it alone. That isolation is real, and it's something many leaders struggle with. The pressure to always perform, the responsibility of guiding others—it can be a lonely road. But it doesn't have to be.

---

*I completely resonate with the sentiment that leadership can often feel isolating. The weight of tough decisions, the pressure to perform, and the responsibility of guiding others can indeed make the journey lonely at times. For years, I embraced the motto "lift as I climb," believing that by helping others along the way, I could elevate both myself and those around me. However, I came to realize that this approach had its limits.*

*I used to assume that everyone I lifted wanted to be part of my ascent and began to indirectly blame them for my own perceived stagnation. This perspective was not only unfair, but also misplaced. I learned that while my desire to support others was genuine, it was unrealistic to expect everyone to share or join me on my unique journey to success. Many may wish to reach their own destinations but aren't necessarily aligned with or interested in my specific path.*

*This realization brought a profound shift in my approach. I understood that lifting others doesn't mean carrying them with me on every step of my journey. Instead, it's about offering support in a way that respects their individual paths and acknowledges my own needs. The period of strategic rest I took to reflect on this was invaluable. It allowed me to recalibrate my expectations and approach, ultimately leading to a more fulfilling and realistic perspective on leadership and collaboration. The rest was indeed worth it, as it clarified how to lead more effectively and sustainably, without feeling alone on the path. - Dr. K*

---

The best leaders understand the power of building supportive networks—mentors, coaches (like Dr. K, also known as "Coach K"), and trusted colleagues who walk alongside you. These relationships aren't just nice to have—they're lifelines. They provide the wisdom, encouragement, and honest feedback you need to keep moving forward with confidence. So, if you ever feel the weight of leadership becoming too heavy, remember: you're not meant to carry it alone. Surround yourself with people who lift you up and help you stay grounded.

At the end of the day, leadership is about nurturing—yourself and others. When you prioritize self-care, invest in your growth, and build strong support systems, you're setting yourself up for long-term success. You're creating a solid foundation that allows you to lead with clarity, creativity, and resilience—no matter the challenges ahead.

*Assess*

**Assess**, the second pillar, is one of the most transformative tools in your personal growth toolkit. When was the last time you truly paused, stepped back, and reflected—not just on your work performance, but on your overall well-being? So often, we get caught in the rush of daily tasks, pushing ourselves to meet expectations without checking in with our most valuable resource: ourselves.

Self-reflection is where it all begins. It's about asking the tough questions: Am I taking care of myself the way I should? Where am I out of balance? Am I really prioritizing rest and well-being, or am I just running on autopilot? The truth is, if you want to live with clarity and purpose, you need to get real about what's working in your life and what's not. By regularly assessing your mental, emotional, and physical health, you set the stage for deeper personal growth and success in all areas of your life.

*Here's the reality*: when you're thriving, everything in your life improves. Your energy, your focus, and your sense of calm radiate outward, influencing your relationships, your work, and your ability to navigate challenges. Self-awareness doesn't just boost your well-being—it enhances how you show up in every aspect of your life. It gives you the foundation to lead yourself with strength and clarity, ensuring that you can handle whatever comes your way.

---

*I've found that the more self-aware I become, the better I lead. When you're in tune with how to manage your stress, you're not just more effective, you're more inspiring. Your team, your family, and your community look to you as someone who not only gets things done but does so with grace and resilience. And that's the kind of leadership that lifts everyone up. When you thrive, you give others permission to thrive too. - Dr. Wilson*

---

But personal growth isn't a solo act. Whether you're managing your own schedule, balancing family obligations, or simply trying to hit personal goals, it's crucial to understand the dynamics that shape your day-to-day life. Are the people in your circle—your family, friends, or colleagues—experiencing stress that's affecting you? Is there a strain in your relationships that you've overlooked? Taking time to assess the flow of your interactions helps you identify areas where you need to adjust. Maybe it's about setting boundaries or offering more support, or maybe it's about making space for your own needs.

Feedback is another powerful tool for self-assessment that's often overlooked. Have you asked the people closest to you—whether they're friends, mentors, or partners—how they feel about your current priorities? Are you taking care of yourself in ways that others notice, or are you quietly wearing yourself down? Honest, reflective input from those who care about you can be a goldmine. It provides you with the clarity to adjust your habits, routines, and commitments so you can create a life that values your well-being as much as your ambitions.

And let's talk about the bigger picture—your life as a whole. Beyond your personal habits, look at the broader environment you're creating. Is your daily schedule supporting your health and happiness, or is it a source of stress? Are you carving out time for rest, hobbies, and the things that truly matter to you? Are you making decisions that align with your core values, or are you just going through the motions?

This is your chance to zoom out and get intentional about how you structure your life. If certain routines or relationships aren't contributing to your well-being, this is your opportunity to make changes. It's not about making radical shifts overnight—it's about taking small, thoughtful steps toward a life that feels balanced and aligned with your needs.

The road to living a balanced, fulfilled life begins with regular self-assessment. By focusing on how you're doing, how you're interacting with the people around you, and how you're shaping your environment, you can make intentional changes that boost your well-being and unlock your full potential. When you prioritize yourself, you're not just improving your life—you're creating the space to thrive. The more you reflect, the more aligned you become with your true self, and the more you'll experience lasting fulfillment and success.

*Prioritize*

**Prioritize** is the third and final element, and it's where the real transformation happens. This is about making rest not just a nice-to-have, but a non-negotiable part of your leadership journey. It's time to move from understanding the importance of rest to actively integrating it into your life.

Setting goals is the first critical step. To truly prioritize strategic rest, you need a roadmap—a structured yet flexible plan that keeps you on track. That's where combining the SMART and HARD goal frameworks comes into play. This blend provides clarity, structure, and deep personal motivation.

Let's start with SMART goals: Specific, Measurable, Achievable, Relevant, and Time-bound.

- **Specific**: Define clear, rest-related objectives. Maybe it's scheduling a 15-minute mindfulness break each afternoon or committing to unplugging from work emails by 7 p.m.
- **Measurable**: Track your progress. Keep a log of how many breaks you take or how many evenings you successfully disconnect from work.
- **Achievable**: Set goals that are realistic given your current workload. Don't aim for eight hours of sleep if you're currently getting five. Start by adding 30 minutes.
- **Relevant**: Ensure your goals align with your leadership effectiveness. Rest should directly contribute to your ability to lead better.
- **Time-bound**: Set deadlines. Perhaps you'll implement these changes over the next month and reassess their impact at the end.

But structure isn't enough—you need passion and commitment. That's where HARD goals come in: Heartfelt, Animated, Required, and Difficult.

- **Heartfelt**: Choose goals that resonate deeply with you. Maybe you want to improve your sleep to have more energy for your family or to reignite a hobby you love.
- **Animated**: Visualize the positive outcomes. Picture yourself leading with vitality, creativity flowing, and feeling truly present in each moment.

- **Required**: Make rest a must-have, not a maybe. Recognize that without rest, your effectiveness and health are at stake.
- **Difficult**: Challenge yourself. Perhaps you'll commit to a tech-free weekend once a month or delegate tasks you've always held onto.

By blending SMART and HARD goals, you're crafting a strategy that's both practical and deeply motivating. You're not just scheduling rest—you're passionately pursuing it as a vital component of your leadership.

Next, you must acknowledge this isn't just about setting goals for your work or life, it's about being intentional with how you allocate your most valuable resources—**your time, energy, and attention**—to prioritize what truly matters: your well-being. When you invest in practices that promote relaxation and balance, you're laying the foundation for sustainable growth, success and leadership.

Start by looking at your **time**. Are you blocking out moments for rest, reflection, and downtime? This might mean scheduling time on your calendar for a morning walk, taking real vacations where you disconnect, or simply carving out time for a quiet lunch where you can pause and recharge. These intentional time investments give you the space to breathe, reset, and return to your day with fresh energy.

Next, think about your **energy**. Are you pouring it into activities that restore you or deplete you? Engaging in things that recharge your spirit—whether it's exercise, spending time in nature, or reading a good book—keeps your energy levels high. The key is to find what nourishes you and make it a non-negotiable part of your routine.

Finally, consider your **attention**. Are you focusing on what truly matters to you, or are distractions hijacking your concentration? Identifying and minimizing these distractions can help you reclaim your focus and channel your attention toward your goals. By prioritizing your time, energy, and attention, you can cultivate a more fulfilling and productive life.

Now, reflect on how you're investing in **support**. Support systems play a crucial role in optimizing time, energy, and attention, ultimately contributing to personal success and well-being. Whether it's seeking out a coach, mentor, or even close friends who uplift you, these relationships remind you that you don't have to do it all alone. By prioritizing these supportive connections, you give yourself the space to grow, recharge, and thrive.

But prioritizing your well-being goes beyond setting time for rest—it's about embracing **communication** with yourself. Be open about your needs and struggles. Share your wins and setbacks with those close to you. This vulnerability fosters deeper connections and encourages others to prioritize their own well-being too. When you start leading your life with rest as a priority, you send a message to those around you: **Rest matters.**

And finally, make rest a part of your **daily routine**. Take regular breaks throughout your day, use your vacation time to fully unplug, and most importantly, listen to your body when it tells you it needs a break. Recognize that rest isn't something you earn after you've worked hard—it's something you deserve because you value your well-being.

By prioritizing rest in all areas of your life, you're not just enhancing your own effectiveness, you're setting yourself up for long-term success. You'll be more energized, focused, and ready to take on challenges with clarity and resilience. **Prioritizing rest** isn't about doing less—it's about showing up fully and intentionally in every part of your life. When you lead with rest as a cornerstone, you empower yourself to be the best version of yourself.

This isn't just about feeling better. It's about living better. Take the step. Make rest the foundation of your personal growth, and your future self will thank you.

Beyond traditional SMART and HARD goals, the **Be-Do-Have** model (discussed by various authors and thought leaders, Stephen Covey, for example) offers a transformative approach to integrating strategic rest into leadership. To apply this model effectively, start by focusing on **who you need to become**: develop self-awareness about your need for rest, cultivate resilience, and be a role model for well-being. Next, concentrate on **what actions you need to take**: schedule regular downtime, practice mindfulness, delegate tasks, and promote a culture that values rest and flexibility. Ultimately, these actions will lead to enhanced productivity through increased energy and focus, improved well-being from reducing stress and preventing burnout, and a positive leadership impact that inspires your team and fosters a balanced, productive work environment. For a more comprehensive guide on applying these principles, see **Appendix E**.

*Practical applications of NAP*

Ready to transform your leadership and well-being? Here are five practical ways to harness the power of the NAP Framework—**Nurture, Assess, Prioritize**—to supercharge your effectiveness:

1. **Establish Your Self-Care Routine**: Take charge of your well-being by creating daily habits that prioritize you. Commit to getting enough sleep, exercising regularly, and nourishing your body with healthy foods. These self-care practices aren't just good for you—they're essential for managing stress and keeping your performance levels high. Imagine facing challenges with renewed energy and a clear mind, ready to lead effectively no matter what comes your way.

2. **Incorporate Mindfulness and Relaxation Techniques**: Make mindfulness your secret weapon. Integrate simple practices like meditation or deep breathing into your daily routine to stay calm and centered. These techniques help you handle stress more effectively, boost your decision-making skills, and sharpen your concentration. The result? A more balanced and impactful leadership style that inspires those around you.

3. **Invest in Your Professional Development**: Become a lifelong learner. Dive into seminars, workshops, or retreats that focus on personal growth and well-being. These experiences are more than educational—they're transformative. You'll gain fresh insights and practical tools to weave well-being practices into your leadership approach, propelling you forward both personally and professionally.

4. **Build Your Support Network**: Surround yourself with people who lift you higher. Seek out mentors

and coaches who offer guidance, support, and a sounding board for your ideas. Don't limit yourself to workplace connections. Expand your network beyond the office to gain new perspectives and invaluable support. These relationships will enrich your journey and open doors you didn't even know existed.

5. **Assess and Improve Your Work Environment**: Take a good look at your work dynamics, task management, and organizational policies related to well-being. Are there opportunities to make things better? Implement stress-reduction techniques, advocate for mental health support, and explore flexible work options. By enhancing your environment, you'll boost productivity and maintain that all-important healthy balance.

By embracing these practical steps, you're not just talking about strategic rest—you're living it. **Prioritize** methods that support sustainable leadership and personal success. **Assess** your time, energy, and attention with honesty, and **nurture** your well-being relentlessly. These actions will pave the way for resilience, heightened productivity, and the profound benefits of strategic rest.

But don't stop here. We've crafted 30 strategies to help you effectively embed **Nurture**, **Assess**, and **Prioritize** in your leadership journey. For each pillar of the NAP Framework, we provide **10 actionable strategies**, each accompanied by an activity, a reflection question, and a practical tip. To dive deeper, turn to **Appendix B** to read this comprehensive list.

Your journey toward enhanced leadership and well-being starts now. Embrace the NAP Framework and watch as you—and those you lead—thrive like never before.

# CHAPTER 4
# STRATEGIC REST IN ACTION

Our personal journeys revealed something profound: the life-changing power of strategic rest. That realization gave birth to the **NAP Framework**—Nurture, Assess, Prioritize. Driven by a shared commitment to both leadership excellence and personal well-being, we discovered how prioritizing rest and self-care transformed not only our effectiveness as professionals, but also as business owners.

We learned that true, sustainable success in leadership requires more than just hard work. It calls for a holistic approach—one that builds mental resilience, enhances decision-making, and sparks creativity. And yes, it demands a willingness to *embrace a dose of disruptive change!*

The **NAP Framework** was designed with this in mind: to help leaders cultivate their well-being, assess their organizational environments, and set priorities that drive long-term success. We didn't just create this framework—we lived it. We used our own experiences navigating tough challenges to shape a practical tool that empowers leaders to thrive.

**This is our story**, and we invite you to discover how the NAP Framework can transform your leadership journey, just as it did for us.

---

*For me, Dr. K, the concept of leadership began to take shape during my college years. In 2006, I eagerly joined Zeta Phi Beta Sorority Inc., diving headfirst into a transformative leadership journey. I embraced every executive role within the chapter, juggling event planning, community outreach, and organizational responsibilities with intense dedication. Amid the flurry of meetings and late-night emails, I experienced a pivotal realization: true strength in leadership lies not just in relentless effort, but in collaboration and recognizing the need to pause, breathe, and recharge.*

*Reflecting on these early experiences, I came to understand that leadership is not a sprint but a marathon. Rest is not a luxury, but a necessity for sustainable success and shared responsibility. This insight, though not explicitly framed as a strategy at the time, became a foundational element of my approach to leadership.*

*I transitioned into my first professional role after earning a master's, where my immersion in residence life at a college meant being constantly responsive to student needs. Despite the support of my colleagues, the weight of being the only Black person in a predominantly white institution was significant. My quest for inclusivity led me to a historically Black university, but I continued to struggle with integrating leadership and rest in a demanding housing role. It wasn't until I moved into an administrative position that I began to intentionally embrace strategic rest. I started to prioritize reflection, self-care, and rejuvenation, which were crucial for nurturing both personal well-being and professional growth.*

*Over the next six years, my focus on assessment extended beyond professional decisions, guiding me to challenge limiting beliefs and define my ideal work culture. The COVID-19 pandemic sparked profound self-reflection, leading me to redefine my spiritual and professional life. This period of introspection inspired the creation of transformative works like "Recharge: A Self-Awareness Approach to Goal Achievement" and "Reclaiming Our Affirmations," which challenged outdated narratives and embraced bold authenticity. I began to set boundaries and prioritize mental health through scheduled self-care.*

*These steps empowered me to redefine leadership through intentional rest and holistic well-being.*

*Today, my approach to leadership reflects a renewed perspective: life's journey should be enjoyed, not endured. I reject burnout as a prerequisite for success and advocate for defining purpose boldly, setting clear boundaries and embracing rest without guilt. By challenging outdated narratives and nurturing a balanced approach to well-being, I demonstrate that effective leadership thrives when grounded in authenticity and strategic self-care. I now cherish the principles of the NAP framework more than ever, having unintentionally woven them into my leadership journey from the very beginning.*

## Dr. K's Approach to NAP

*Nurture.* When it comes to nurturing strategic rest in my leadership routine, I've got a few go-to strategies. For starters, I use Calendly.com to manage my schedule, and I make it a point to block out time every day for lunch. I also carve out at least two hours between 9 a.m. and 5 p.m. to just unwind or rest. Even though I work from home now, I started this practice in a previous administrative role, and it's been a game-changer. It's all about balancing how much I give to others with how much I give to myself.

A great example of how this approach has positively impacted my leadership is that it has made a difference in my ability to manage stress. As both a business owner and a professor, I often juggle multiple responsibilities and deal with situations where it seems like everyone needs something from me all at once (which, let's be honest, happens a lot). But because I've built strategic rest and self-care into my routine, I don't get as stressed or overwhelmed. I handle these busy times with a lot more ease and clarity, which helps

---

me stay focused and effective, whether I'm managing a business or teaching a class.

For mindfulness and wellness, I keep things simple but effective. I take a few moments throughout the day to pause and do deep breathing exercises—just three breaths, but done slowly and intentionally. I also believe in the power of actual naps or just lying down to recharge. And for a five-month stretch, I worked with a stretch coach who taught me how crucial it is to stretch regularly. I found that keeping my body flexible has a direct impact on how I lead, both personally and professionally.

Investing in professional development for me means investing in personal development. This includes things like working with a stretch coach, getting monthly massages, and hitting the gym three to four times a week. Sure, it costs money, but it's worth it. This investment has helped me feel less anxious and has allowed me to make better decisions. It's also sharpened my transformational leadership style, making me more effective and empathetic as a leader.

*Assess.* As an assessment professional, I take a meticulous approach to evaluating and refining my rest and mindfulness practices. While I may not always achieve the same level of precision as in formal assessments, I remain committed to regular, thoughtful review. Each Sunday, I examine my calendar thoroughly to plan for the upcoming week, making strategic adjustments to ensure I carve out ample time for rest and recharging.

My energy is paramount, and I guard it diligently. I am highly attuned to how different tasks and events impact my energy levels and the time required to complete them. By closely monitoring these variables, I can assess the effectiveness of my practices and make necessary adjustments to optimize my well-being.

Recharging is not just a necessity but a cherished pastime for me. I prioritize it as a fundamental part of my routine, recognizing its vital role in maintaining my overall effectiveness and balance. This careful stewardship of my energy ensures that I remain at my best, both personally and professionally.

A notable example of addressing a challenge in this area happened in the summer of 2024. I was deeply immersed in reading dissertations while serving as a chair and committee member. With no vacation and a constant workload, I found myself completely exhausted by the end of August. Despite the short turnaround time needed to plan for the fall semester classes, I had to make the tough decision to cancel meetings, events, and travel plans to give myself the silence and space I needed to recharge. I remember telling a colleague, "I can't do this, I need to step away." Even though it was difficult, especially given the impending start of the new semester, I had to respect the data and make changes. This decision not only restored my personal effectiveness but also ensured that I could contribute more meaningfully in the upcoming semester.

*Prioritize*. In 2024, I invested in an executive coaching program with the Meta Performance™ Institute from February to July. This experience was a real eye-opener about how crucial rest is to achieving my vision, which focuses on leaving a lasting legacy. With this insight, I set a HARD goal for myself: to schedule and take at least three non business-related trips by the end of the year, ensuring that each trip included a minimum of four days dedicated to rest and relaxation.

This goal was deeply heartfelt. It wasn't just about taking breaks, but about truly integrating rest into my entrepreneurial life. The goal was also animated, combining work with downtime. I saw these trips as opportunities for both professional growth and personal recharging, making the process dynamic and engaging.

Balancing intense work with effective rest is necessary for me as a solo entrepreneur. It's vital to prevent burnout and keep productivity levels high. Planning and executing these trips while ensuring they include proper rest presented a significant challenge, requiring considerable effort and organization, especially when managing everything on my own.

I must admit, I set this goal while writing this book. So, if you're curious about my progress, connect with me on Instagram (@disruptnarratives) to follow my journey. I'm always reminding people to prioritize rest and find what truly works for them. Life is a personal race, and it's important to run at your own pace and take breaks when needed. I'm incredibly grateful for the support from colleagues, family, and friends—even if that support means accepting my crazy idea of writing a book on strategic rest in leadership with me! A big thanks to Erin for being part of this journey.

---

*For me, Dr. Wilson, breaking free from the belief that hard work must always feel exhausting took years of unlearning. Even before I entered grade school, the phrase 'hard work' was used interchangeably with 'success' and 'productivity' during those critical formative years. I grew up believing that if work was not hard, it was not done right. Successful people, I was taught, were the ones who stayed up late and woke up early.*

*Yet, there was another narrative quietly unfolding in the background of my childhood. Growing up in the Seventh-day Adventist faith, I was introduced to the transformative power of rest. In my faith, rest is not just a luxury, it is a divine gift, a principle woven into the fabric of creation. The idea that God created for six days and rested on the seventh is a cornerstone of our beliefs. I watched my parents embrace this concept of strategic rest, taking long, peaceful Sabbath naps, moving slowly through their Saturdays, and prioritizing meaningful connections over endless productivity. I did not realize it at the time, but these moments were planting seeds, helping me understand that rest is not the enemy of productivity, it's the fuel.*

*But when I got to college, I began to stray from the lessons I had learned about rest. The constant juggling of coursework, extracurriculars, jobs, and social events left me running on fumes. Yet, the more I stretched myself thin, the more praise I received. Everyone around me seemed to celebrate my ability to do it all. This unhealthy relationship with busyness was constantly reinforced. More opportunities, more leadership roles, more meetings—all seemed like stepping stones to a successful future. I wore my exhaustion like a badge of honor, a sign that I was worthy of the good things coming my way.*

*Then, after graduate school, my obsession with constant motion spiraled out of control. Driven by ambition, I worked long hours, priding myself on being the last one left in the office, and responding to emails at all hours. I said 'yes' to every project, every opportunity that seemed like a shortcut to the next level. I filled my weekends with clubs and organizations, all while trying to be a good wife to my new husband. I was burning the candle at both ends, and then, suddenly, the bottom fell out. Years of running at full speed finally caught up with me and I experienced my first stress-induced seizure.*

*That moment was a wake-up call. It forced me to confront everything I was doing, to make some hard choices about what truly mattered in my life. It was time to rethink the narrative I had been living and redefine what success looks like for me.*

*My journey into understanding my priorities and diving deep into self-awareness taught me a powerful truth: I am valuable, even when I am not embodying the image of the overworked woman who seems to have it all. This inner work revealed that constant movement is not the same as true productivity. I discovered that to do the work I am called to do, I need moments to recharge, and I have released the guilt around pausing with purpose. Now, I embrace rest as a meaningful act, knowing it allows me to return as the best version of myself.*

*With fresh eyes, I began to see a pattern: the most effective leaders and the truly successful people around me were not the ones who were always exhausted or complaining endlessly about how busy they were. No, it was those who carved out time for vacations, who set firm boundaries to protect their time, and who understood the immense value of investing in convenience to enhance their lives. They were not just managing their time, they were reclaiming their energy and joy. It became clear that success was not about doing more, but about doing what mattered most, with intention and clarity.*

*Experiencing the transformative power of strategic and intentional rest, I felt a deep urge to share this gift with others. I wanted people to understand that rest is not a luxury, it is a vital key to success. This passion led me and my colleague, Dr. K, to develop the NAP framework, a simple yet powerful approach designed to help people give themselves permission to rest and recognize it as one of the most meaningful tools for achieving their fullest potential.*

## Dr. Wilson's Approach to NAP

*Nurture.* Building nurturing networks centered around strategic rest has been a game changer for both my work and my personal life. I've learned that creating spaces where I can be vulnerable and authentic—rather than always presenting a polished, unapproachable front—allows me to genuinely care for my emotional and mental health. The truth is, you can't just wait for these moments of rest and safe spaces to appear magically, you must create them.

I've woven these spaces into my leadership routine in many ways, but two practices stand out. The first is my monthly strategy call with Dr. K. While most might view a virtual call as another piece of work, our calls are anything but. This is where I get to share how I've grown over the past month, hold myself accountable for the goals I've set, and freely bounce off ideas that I might not feel comfortable sharing elsewhere. These calls are more than just strategy sessions—they're healing spaces. No topic is off-limits. We follow our spirits where they lead, tossing aside any strict agenda in favor of deep, meaningful conversation. There are tears, there are laughs, and there's magic in the messiness. New strategies emerge, new plans take shape, and I leave each call feeling recharged, rested, and ready to conquer another month.

The second way I create these nurturing spaces is by committing to a quarterly retreat with a talented colleague and dear friend who also owns a consulting firm. We choose a hotel within an hour's drive from our city, eliminating the stress of airports and long-distance travel. Once we check in, we tie up any loose work ends and then the real retreat begins—a full 24 hours dedicated to strategic rest and rejuvenation. Over dinner at a restaurant we've never tried before, we dive deep into conversations about our business goals, celebrate our wins, and analyze our setbacks. We share best practices, offer advice, and reflect on how we can support each other in the months ahead.

After dinner, we leave room for spontaneity, often finding ourselves networking organically in the hotel lobby or wherever the night takes us. The next morning is intentionally slow-paced, providing space to rest and reset. By mid-afternoon, we wrap up with lunch and a final review of the goals we've set, ensuring we're aligned and accountable. I always leave these retreats feeling refocused, relaxed, and ready to make big things happen for myself, my family, and my business.

These practices aren't just good for my soul, they've made me a more effective leader. When I'm well-rested and grounded, I'm better able to make clear-headed decisions, communicate effectively, and lead with empathy. I prioritize self-care because I know it's not a luxury—it's a necessity. It's about recognizing that my well-being directly impacts my ability to lead others.

To promote mindfulness and wellness in my own life, I set intentional goals that blend professional growth with personal care. For example, I've committed to attending at least two professional development events each year that incorporate aspects of self-care and mindfulness. These could be retreats, workshops, or seminars where I learn new skills, but also where there is space to reflect, recharge, and connect with like-minded leaders. By investing in experiences that prioritize both learning and wellness, I'm reminded that personal growth fuels professional excellence.

This investment in self-care has profoundly influenced my leadership style. I've learned to lead from a place of balance, not burnout. I prioritize clarity and calm over chaos and urgency. I've become more strategic in decision-making, less reactive, and more thoughtful about how I spend my time and energy. My leadership is now anchored in the understanding that rest is not a reward you get after hard work—it's the fuel that makes everything else possible. And this shift, this commitment to nurturing my well-being, has made all the difference in my effectiveness as a leader.

*Assess.* Taking time to assess my needs is one of the most powerful tools in my quest for balance and effectiveness. I start each day, even before my feet hit the floor, with a simple prayer. Then, I map out what needs to happen for me to feel accomplished and aligned that day. Most people stop at planning their tasks, but I go further—I also think intentionally about what I need for rest. If I haven't slept well, I prioritize getting to bed early that night. If I know my morning is packed, I make every effort to keep my afternoon lighter. This daily assessment helps me stay attuned to my body's needs and ensures I'm not just moving through my day, but moving through it well-rested.

At the beginning of the third week of each month, I conduct a deeper assessment. I sit down with my Remarkable 2 and map out my entire upcoming month. I put every engagement, personal and professional, into a single calendar. I literally draw a calendar that centers around my well-being first, using one of the templates, and then move things around digitally to make sure rest is prioritized. Most people don't think of combining work and rest on the same page, but for me, it's like choreographing a dance where both elements move in sync. It's a delicate balance, but one that makes all the difference in how I show up each day.

I've also learned to protect my weekends fiercely. My goal is to avoid packing them so full that I return on Monday feeling more drained than when I started. I've discovered that saying 'no' to Friday commitments has been a game changer. I block off Friday evenings for myself—just me, my husband, a few close friends, or my favorite quiet activities. This dedicated time allows me to recharge, so even if my weekends fill up, I've already invested in rest. It's my way of ensuring that I can be present and productive even on non-work days.

When I know I have a busy weekend ahead, I take intentional steps to protect my energy for the following week. I might make Monday a remote day, or when I worked in a role that required me to be in the office, I would block out Monday mornings in my Outlook calendar. No meetings, no distractions—just time for me to handle the essential administrative tasks that set me up for success. This small adjustment increased my weekly productivity significantly by allowing me to ease into my workweek with focus and clarity.

To assess the effectiveness of my rest and mindfulness practices, I pay close attention to how I feel—physically, mentally, and emotionally. If I notice fatigue, irritability, or difficulty focusing, these are red flags that my balance is off. I ask myself key questions: Am I feeling rested when I wake up? Do I feel a sense of calm or control throughout my day? If the answer is no, I take that as a sign that I need to adjust my schedule.

One time, I realized I was constantly feeling drained by Wednesday. My calendar was packed with back-to-back meetings and heavy tasks at the beginning of each week. I decided to make a shift: I moved some of my more demanding tasks to later in the week and started blocking time for midday breaks on Tuesdays and Wednesdays. The result was immediate—I felt more energized, more focused, and my productivity improved. That experience taught me that a successful balance isn't static—it's something I must continually assess and adjust to meet my needs.

For me, the metrics of success aren't just about how much I get done but about how I feel while doing it. Am I moving through my day with ease and clarity? Do I feel restored, or am I running on fumes? Rest isn't just a break, it's the foundation that allows everything else to thrive. By being mindful, intentional, and strategic about rest, I'm able to show up fully for myself and others, day after day.

*Prioritize.* When I ask people about their priorities, they usually list things like family, work, fitness, or wealth. But what if I told you that making time to do nothing should be a priority, too? For me, it absolutely is. Building in time to do nothing creates space for new ideas to flourish, for creativity to flow, for learning to happen, and for reconnecting with friends or reimagining the outcomes I want. I have learned that being intentional about leaving time for nothing actually drives me to be more purposeful and productive during the moments when I am moving.

I have also learned that prioritizing rest and mindfulness means getting comfortable with the word 'No.' Not every event requires my presence, not every client aligns with my skills. I don't have to be all things to all people. True prioritization begins with intentionally deciding when to be available and when to protect my time. It is about prioritizing the activities and tasks that will move me toward the goals and outcomes I have in mind.

To put this into practice, I set SMART goals around rest and mindfulness. For example, one of my goals was to create a minimum of three blocks of 'white space'—time with no scheduled activities—each week. I measured this by tracking my calendar to ensure these spaces remained untouched. The goal was achievable and relevant because I needed this time to recharge, and I set a timeline to reassess every month to see if it was working.

Early in my consulting career, before implementing the NAP framework, I fell into the trap of trying to be everything to everyone. Need a coach? I'm your girl. Want a strategic plan for your department? Sure, hire me. Need someone to create a social media page? I love social media, pick me! This 'golden retriever' energy left me buried under hours of work I did not even enjoy, all outside of my already packed schedule. I'd promised myself that my consulting work would be work I loved, but my need to please everyone was pushing me to the brink of burnout.

That's when I set another SMART goal: to identify the type of consulting work that truly brought me joy and to focus on it exclusively. I realized that what energized me most was facilitating professional development for teams and cohorts during staff retreats. So, I made a conscious choice: I would prioritize clients who wanted that kind of work and refer those asking for other services to colleagues who specialized in those areas. My goal was specific and measurable—I wanted at least 80 percent of my consulting work to focus on facilitating training for teams by the end of the year. It was achievable because I already had a network and the skills, it was relevant because it aligned with my purpose, and it was time-bound with a clear deadline.

And it worked. Now, without much advertising, my clients come from referrals—people who say they can feel the joy and energy when I'm presenting because it is clear I love what I do. And they're right. Time seems to disappear when I'm facilitating sessions. Getting paid to do this work feels like icing on the cake, but it all started with saying no to the work that did not align with my purpose and focusing on what truly mattered to me.

I also began setting goals around the people I invested my time in. I made a conscious effort to spend time with those who energized me, not those who drained me. We often think that every invitation, every 'let me pick your brain' request, requires a 'yes.' But no is a powerful answer, too. 'Send me an email about that.' 'I'm not free now, but I can find time later.' These are all valid responses that use boundaries to help you prioritize. Use them! The sooner you start saying no to what does not serve you, the sooner you will experience the restorative power of strategic rest and mindful living.

We encourage leaders to reflect extensively on how they can integrate the NAP Framework principles—Nurture, Assess, and Prioritize—into their leadership tactics to support restful behaviors and promote well-being within their personal and professional spaces. Through our own accounts, we shed light on the transforming process of incorporating strategic rest into leadership. Leaders who put their own well-being first and foster a culture that values resilience and balance not only increase their own effectiveness but also foster an atmosphere where people flourish. In the end, our collective experiences highlight how crucial it is to embrace leisure as a cornerstone of sustainable leadership, forming corporate cultures that place a premium on resilience, long-term success, and wellness. *We look forward to all the ways you NAP in leadership!*

# CHAPTER 5
# EMBRACING THE POWER OF
## STRATEGIC REST

In the fast-paced world of leadership, where expectations are sky-high and demands never seem to slow down, the concept of strategic relaxation often gets lost. Yet, through our own experiences, we've come to understand that incorporating rest into leadership strategies isn't just a nice-to-have—it's a non-negotiable for long-term success and well-being. In this chapter, we'll dive into how prioritizing rest and fostering a resilient culture can transform your leadership approach, all through the lens of the **NAP Framework: Nurture, Assess, Prioritize**.

Our journey began like many leaders—caught in the relentless grind, believing that the key to success was constant effort. The more we worked, the more we thought we'd achieve. But as we pushed ourselves to the brink, we realized something crucial: true effectiveness and sustained success don't come from running on empty. They come from balance, from embracing deliberate downtime, and from investing in self-care.

That's when we shifted our mindset. We understood that for leadership to thrive, it must include moments of pause, reflection, and recovery. With this newfound understanding, we created the **NAP Framework**—a structured approach that helps leaders nurture their personal well-being, assess the dynamics of their teams and organizations, and prioritize projects that drive meaningful progress.

This framework isn't theoretical, it's a practical guide that reshaped how we lead, and it can do the same for you. By the end of this chapter, you'll see how strategic rest is the secret weapon that can elevate both your leadership and your life.

**Implementation: Putting Framework into Practice**

To truly bring the **NAP Framework** to life, leaders must lead by example. It's not enough to just talk about strategic rest—you must live it. This means actively practicing rest in your own life while championing it for your team. When you, as a leader, model behaviors like taking regular breaks, prioritizing time off, and genuinely supporting your team's well-being, you create a ripple effect. You set the tone for a culture where self-care isn't an afterthought—it's a priority.

Imagine the impact when your team sees you stepping away for a mental reset or encouraging them to take the time they need to recharge. You're not just managing people, you're empowering them to lead healthier, more balanced lives. And that's where true success begins—because when well-being is prioritized, everyone thrives.

In **Appendix C**, we introduce our 21-Day Strategic Rest Action Plan, crafted using the NAP framework. This plan outlines how integrating intentional rest practices can profoundly impact your leadership journey.

*Nurture: Prioritizing Personal Well-Being*

The first pillar of the **NAP Framework**, **Nurture**, is all about prioritizing your well-being and self-care. As a leader, it's easy to fall into the trap of thinking that powering through is the only way to succeed. But true leadership isn't just about how much you do—it's about how well you take care of yourself so you can lead with clarity and strength.

We encourage you to build daily routines that include mindfulness practices, regular exercise, and, yes, enough sleep. These habits are game changers. They don't just improve your physical health—they sharpen your mental resilience, giving you the energy and focus to make smarter decisions and tackle challenges with grace and composure. When you nurture yourself, you're not just surviving the grind—you're thriving in it, setting an example for those around you.

*Assess: Personalized Approach to Work Dynamics*

The second pillar of the **NAP Framework**, **Assess**, is all about taking a deeper look at the dynamics of your leadership—how stress, workload, and team interactions are playing out in real time. It's easy to get caught up in the day-to-day grind and miss the warning signs of burnout or imbalance, but this pillar pushes you to be proactive.

Regular check-ins with your team—whether through surveys, feedback sessions, or open conversations—offer you invaluable insights into what's really going on beneath the surface. Are your team members feeling overwhelmed? Are there hidden stressors or inefficiencies dragging everyone down? When you actively assess these factors, you're not just reacting to problems as they arise—you're preventing them from taking root in the first place.

By taking this approach, you're creating a workplace that doesn't just survive under pressure, but thrives. You'll foster a culture of balance, productivity, and well-being that supports not only your success but the sustained success of your entire team.

*Prioritize: Setting Strategic Goals*

The final pillar of the **NAP Framework**, **Prioritize**, is about bringing your goals into alignment with your personal values and well-being. It's not just about getting more done—it's about focusing on what truly matters to you in a way that supports a balanced and fulfilling life.

Start by weaving in practices that help you manage both your work and personal life more effectively. Think about setting flexible work hours or designing a schedule that gives you room to honor your personal commitments. Make your mental health non-negotiable by building a solid support system—whether it's through self-care routines, therapy, or spending time with friends and family who lift you up.

But don't stop there. Prioritizing also means investing in your own growth. Pursue learning opportunities that excite you—take that online course, attend that workshop, or dive into a new hobby. Continuous learning doesn't just develop your skills—it keeps you engaged, energized, and motivated.

By focusing on initiatives that align with both your goals and your well-being, you're making a powerful statement: success isn't just about what you accomplish, it's about how you grow along the way. You're not only achieving more—you're thriving in every sense.

### Embracing Strategic Rest as a Leadership Imperative

To put it simply, the **NAP Framework** is a leadership game changer. When you understand that **strategic rest** is not just a luxury, but an essential part of effective leadership, everything changes. By focusing on **nurturing your personal well-being**, **assessing the dynamics** in your organization, and **prioritizing what truly matters**, you unlock the potential for sustainable success. You're not just ticking off tasks—you're leading with intention, building a resilient, energized, and thriving culture around you.

Imagine a work environment where leaders and teams don't burn out but instead fuel each other's creativity, energy, and growth. When you adopt strategic rest as part of your leadership style, that's exactly what you create. You're not only more effective—you're a leader who inspires others to thrive alongside you.

The truth is, leadership isn't about how fast you can go or how many hours you can put in. It's about building the right foundation for long-term success—for yourself and for your team. The NAP Framework gives you the tools to do just that. You'll cultivate resilience, maintain clarity under pressure, and prioritize what matters most. By leading with balance and intention, you create space for true growth, innovation, and lasting impact.

So, the question is: are you ready to change the way you lead? The **NAP Framework** invites you to step into a new kind of leadership—one grounded in strategic rest, resilience, and clarity. It's not just about doing more; it's about doing what matters, with purpose and intention.

You're standing on the edge of a transformative journey, one that will elevate your leadership and your life. Embrace the power of **Nurture, Assess, Prioritize**, and watch as you—and your organization—soar to new heights.

# Chapter 6
# Collective Strategic Rest

In our journey through leadership and strategic rest (or what many call well-being), we have come to a powerful realization: strategic rest isn't just about you, and it isn't confined to the people you work with day in and day out. It goes far beyond conventional team dynamics.

Collective strategic rest is about weaving intentional rest practices into the fabric of any collaborative network you consider your "team." And here's the beauty of it: your team isn't just the people in your office or immediate work circle. We invite you to ensure your team is a diverse mix of individuals from different sectors—mentors who guide you, peers in mastermind groups, or even friends and family who share your values and goals.

When you take a collective approach to rest, you're doing more than just prioritizing your own well-being—you're creating a ripple effect. You're ensuring that everyone in your network values and integrates rest, which elevates both your personal effectiveness and the synergy of the entire group. The result? A support system that's not only driven but also resilient, refreshed, and ready to tackle challenges with renewed energy.

## Integrating Grandmother's Safety into Collective Strategic Rest

In our exploration of strategic rest in leadership, Dr. Wilson and I (Dr. K) engaged in a profound conversation about the intersection of rest and safety, sparked by my reading of

Ashley Neese's *Permission to Rest*. This book brought to light the notion that rest is deeply intertwined with feelings of safety, a concept that resonated deeply with us both. I posed the question (and I pose the same question to you, the reader, for reflection)—As you think about your younger self, when did you feel most safe?

Dr. Wilson shared with me that the place where she felt most secure as a child was nestled in her grandmother's lap while she sat in her recliner. Reflecting on this memory, Dr. Wilson realized how rare and precious that sense of safety has become in her life. It struck her that she might never experience such profound security again, highlighting just how integral that feeling of safety is to our ability to rest.

I responded by sharing my own experiences. I recalled how my grandmother's home was a sanctuary of safety during my childhood. Reflecting on this, I admitted that I hadn't fully appreciated this comfort at the time but recognized its significance in hindsight. Since my paternal grandmother (*Geraldine Dixon*) passed away in 2013, I struggled to find genuine rest. The support and acceptance I received from my grandmother allowed me to simply be, without the pressures of performance. Now, the shift towards a performance-driven mindset has made it challenging for me to find the same sense of ease and security.

Our conversation underscored a critical realization: if rest is fundamentally tied to safety, then recreating or accessing that deep sense of security is essential for leaders seeking to achieve sustainable well-being. The loss of our grandmothers, who provided us with unparalleled comfort and acceptance, has illuminated the profound impact such foundational relationships have on our ability to rest. Integrating these insights into our discussion about strategic rest emphasizes the importance of creating environments where leaders can experience similar levels of safety and support. It's about fostering spaces where leaders can not only excel but also find the deep rest and reassurance that were once so effortlessly provided by those who deeply cared for us.

Incorporating these reflections into our understanding of strategic rest reveals a broader, collective dimension. The sense of safety and profound rest we experienced with our grandmothers highlights the importance of creating environments where such feelings can be collectively nurtured. When leaders and their teams experience a shared sense of safety and support, it fosters a culture of collective strategic rest. This approach not only benefits individuals but also enhances overall organizational well-being. By embedding principles of safety and acceptance into the fabric of workplace culture, organizations can cultivate an environment where everyone—leaders and team members alike—feels supported and valued. This collective strategic rest creates a foundation for more sustainable performance, creativity, and resilience, demonstrating that individuals' well-being is deeply interconnected with the health of the entire organization.

Collective strategic rest is a powerful, adaptable way to enhance both your leadership and your well-being. It's about expanding your idea of a "team" to include a diverse range of people—whether they're mentors, peers from different industries, or members of mastermind groups—who share your commitment to growth and balance. By embracing this broader definition, you foster a collective commitment to well-being that strengthens connections and builds resilience within your network.

We have seen firsthand how this flexible approach creates a more connected and effective support system. It's not just about taking care of yourself—it's about creating a shared environment that lifts everyone up, leading to greater success and deeper satisfaction.

Every year, we dedicate ourselves to a practice that has become the foundation of our leadership philosophy and a key driver behind the writing of this book. Our approach to **Collective Strategic Rest**, outlined in **Appendix D**, has been a cornerstone of our strategy, focusing on intentional, rejuvenating, and purposeful connections with one another. This practice has transformed how we lead, offering us invaluable insights into weaving strategic rest into leadership, and we're excited to share our approach with you.

# APPENDIX:
# RESOURCES AND TOOLS

# Appendix A

# Strategic Rest Readiness Assessment

**Purpose:** This assessment will help you gauge your current readiness to effectively integrate the NAP Framework—Nurture, Assess, Prioritize—into your leadership practice. By identifying your strengths and areas for improvement, you can better focus your efforts on achieving strategic rest and enhancing both your performance and well-being.

**Instructions:** For each statement below, rate yourself on a scale from 1 to 5, where:

- **1** = Strongly Disagree
- **2** = Disagree
- **3** = Neutral
- **4** = Agree
- **5** = Strongly Agree

| Statement | Rating |
|---|---|
| 1. I regularly engage in activities that promote my physical well-being (e.g., exercise, healthy eating). | _____ |
| 2. I prioritize my mental and emotional health through practices like mindfulness or therapy. | _____ |
| 3. I am committed to ongoing professional development to enhance my leadership skills. | _____ |
| 4. I actively build and maintain a support network of colleagues, mentors, and peers. | _____ |

5. I set aside time for personal hobbies and interests that contribute to my overall satisfaction. _____

6. I regularly reflect on my current stress levels and emotional state. _____

7. I take time to identify and address any burnout symptoms I might be experiencing. _____

8. I regularly evaluate my work-life balance and make adjustments as needed. _____

9. I seek feedback from others to understand how I am performing and feeling in my role. _____

10. I am proactive in identifying and addressing any personal or professional challenges. _____

11. I have clear, actionable goals that include elements of rest and self-care. _____

12. I effectively allocate time and resources to activities that contribute to my well-being. _____

13. I make a conscious effort to balance high-priority tasks with necessary rest periods. _____

14. I set and track SMART goals related to both professional achievements and personal well-being. _____

15. I integrate HARD goals that reflect my deepest passions and long-term aspirations into my routine. _____

## Scoring

**Step 1:** Calculate your total score for each pillar by adding the scores of the relevant statements.

- **Nurture Total Score:** Sum of statements 1-5
- **Assess Total Score:** Sum of statements 6-10
- **Prioritize Total Score:** Sum of statements 11-15

| | |
|---|---|
| Total Nurture Score: | _____ |
| Total Assess Score: | _____ |
| Total Prioritize Score: | _____ |

**Step 2:** Calculate the overall score by adding the totals from each pillar.

- **Overall Score:** Nurture Total Score + Assess Total Score + Prioritize Total Score

| | |
|---|---|
| Overall Score (N+A+P): | _____ |

## Interpretation of Results

- **Nurture Score:**
    - **15-20:** High readiness. You are effectively nurturing yourself and your professional growth.
    - **10-14:** Moderate readiness. Consider focusing more on self-care and building your support network.
    - **Below 10:** Low readiness. Prioritize enhancing your self-care and professional development efforts.
- **Assess Score:**

- **15-20:** High readiness. You are assessing your well-being effectively and making necessary adjustments.
- **10-14:** Moderate readiness. Increase efforts in regular self-reflection and seeking feedback.
- **Below 10:** Low readiness. Focus on developing a consistent routine for self-assessment and addressing burnout.
- **Prioritize Score:**
  - **15-20:** High readiness. You are successfully prioritizing rest and well-being alongside your goals.
  - **10-14:** Moderate readiness. Review how you allocate time and resources to ensure rest is a priority.
  - **Below 10:** Low readiness. Revise your approach to setting and achieving goals that incorporate rest and self-care.

**Overall Score:**

- **45-60:** Excellent. You are well on your way to effectively integrating strategic rest into your leadership.
- **30-44:** Good. You are making progress but may need to focus on specific areas to enhance your readiness.
- **Below 30:** Needs Improvement. Significant focus is needed to integrate strategic rest effectively into your leadership practice.

**Next Steps:** Based on your scores, identify key areas for development. Use the NAP Framework to guide your efforts in nurturing, assessing, and prioritizing strategic rest in your leadership journey. Refer to the detailed strategies in Appendix B for actionable steps and practical tips to enhance your readiness and overall well-being.

# Appendix B

# 30 Strategies for Using NAP

We've developed a robust set of strategies designed to enhance your leadership journey through effective Nurturing, Assessing, and Prioritizing. Our expanded framework provides you with actionable strategies to fortify each pillar, ensuring you have the tools to thrive.

**Instructions**

1.  **Explore the NAP Framework**: Familiarize yourself with the three core pillars: Nurture, Assess, and Prioritize. Each pillar is crucial for effective leadership and personal growth.
2.  **Access the Strategies**: For each pillar, we've outlined 10 actionable strategies. Each strategy includes:

    o **Activity**: A hands-on task to apply the strategy in a practical context.

    o **Reflection Question**: A prompt to encourage deep thinking and self-assessment.

    o **Practical Tip**: A straightforward piece of advice to help you implement the strategy more effectively.

# NURTURE *Your Rest*

## Introduction to Nurturing Strategic Rest

**Overview**: Nurturing strategic rest involves intentionally incorporating practices into your routine that support effective rest and recovery. It's about creating habits and environments that enhance your ability to recharge, maintain well-being, and sustain peak performance over time. This proactive approach ensures that rest is not an afterthought but a fundamental component of your leadership strategy.

### Reflection Question:

- How can integrating intentional rest practices into your daily routine improve your overall leadership effectiveness and personal well-being?

**Tip**:

- Start by identifying specific areas in your routine where rest can be incorporated or improved. Establish consistent habits and create environments that promote relaxation, making strategic rest a seamless part of your leadership practice.

# Create a Dedicated Rest Space

**Activity:**

- Design and organize a dedicated relaxation space. Choose a comfortable chair, add soft lighting, and include elements like calming artwork or plants.

**Reflection Question:**

- How does having a designated area for relaxation affect your ability to unwind and separate from work?

**Tip:**

- Set up a comfortable, quiet space in your home or office specifically for rest and rejuvenation to enhance your ability to relax and recharge.

## Implement Regular Breaks Throughout the Day

**Activity:**

- Use a timer or app to schedule and take short breaks every 60-90 minutes during work hours. Use these breaks for stretching, walking, or a quick mindfulness exercise.

**Reflection Question:**

- How does taking scheduled breaks impact your productivity and stress levels during work hours?

**Tip:**

- Incorporate brief, frequent breaks into your daily schedule using techniques like the Pomodoro Technique to maintain focus and reduce stress.

# Practice Mindfulness and Relaxation Techniques

**Activity**:

- Set aside 5-10 minutes each day for a mindfulness exercise, such as guided meditation or deep breathing. Use a meditation app or follow online videos.

**Reflection Question**:

- What benefits have you experienced from regularly practicing mindfulness or relaxation exercises in your leadership role?

**Tip**:

- Allocate a few minutes each day for mindfulness practices such as meditation, deep breathing, or progressive muscle relaxation to improve mental clarity and resilience.

# Set Boundaries Between Work and Personal Life

**Activity:**

- Create a clear end-of-workday ritual, such as shutting down your computer, turning off work notifications, or setting a physical boundary like closing your office door.

**Reflection Question:**

- How do clear boundaries between work and personal time contribute to your overall well-being and leadership effectiveness?

**Tip:**

- Establish and adhere to specific work hours and personal time to ensure a healthy balance and to prevent burnout.

# Schedule Downtime and Leisure Activities

**Activity:**

- Plan and calendar at least one leisure activity or hobby each week, such as attending a class, engaging in a sport, or having a social outing.

**Reflection Question:**

- How does regularly engaging in leisure activities and hobbies influence your overall productivity and stress levels?

**Tip:**

- Plan and prioritize leisure activities and personal interests regularly to maintain a balanced life and enhance creativity and relaxation.

# Engage in Regular Physical Activity

**Activity:**

- Develop a weekly exercise routine, including activities such as jogging, cycling, or joining a fitness class. Track your workouts using an app or journal.

**Reflection Question:**

- How has incorporating regular exercise into your routine impacted your stress management and leadership performance?

**Tip:**

- Include at least 30 minutes of physical activity most days of the week, such as walking, jogging, or yoga to support physical and mental well-being.

# Limit Exposure to Work-Related Content During Downtime

**Activity**:

- Set specific times to check and respond to work emails or messages and avoid doing so outside these times. Create a 'do not disturb' schedule for personal rest periods.

**Reflection Question**:

- How does reducing engagement with work-related content during your rest periods affect your mental recovery and overall leadership effectiveness?

**Tip**:

- Avoid checking emails or handling work tasks during designated rest times to fully detach and rejuvenate.

## Create a Pre-Rest Ritual

**Activity:**

- Develop and follow a pre-rest routine, such as reading a chapter of a book, doing gentle stretches, or practicing gratitude journaling to signal the end of your workday.

**Reflection Question:**

- How does having a structured pre-rest routine help you transition from work mode to relaxation more effectively?

**Tip:**

- Develop a calming pre-rest ritual, such as reading a book, taking a warm bath, or listening to relaxing music, to prompt your body and mind to unwind.

# Foster Social Connections and Support Networks

**Activity:**

- Schedule regular catch-ups or networking sessions with friends, mentors, or peers. Use these opportunities to share experiences, seek advice, and provide support.

**Reflection Question:**

- How does maintaining meaningful social connections and support networks contribute to your overall well-being and leadership effectiveness?

**Tip:**

- Actively cultivate relationships with friends, mentors, or peers outside of work to provide emotional support and enhance your resilience.

## Encourage Team-Wide Rest Practices

**Activity**:

- Organize and lead a workshop or team meeting focused on the importance of rest and well-being. Share best practices and create a culture of support for strategic rest.

**Reflection Question**:

- How does promoting and supporting rest practices among your team members affect team cohesion and overall performance?

**Tip**:

- Advocate for and model strategic rest practices within your team, creating a culture that values and supports well-being and work-life balance.

# **ASSESS** *Your Rest*

## **Introduction to Assessing Strategic Rest**

**Overview:** Assessing strategic rest in leadership involves evaluating how well rest practices support leadership effectiveness and personal well-being. This section introduces methods for assessing the impact of strategic rest and its integration into leadership roles.

**Reflection Question:**
- How does assessing your rest practices help you understand their impact on your leadership and overall effectiveness?

**Tip:**
- Effective assessment of rest practices ensures that you maintain optimal performance and prevent burnout by aligning rest strategies with leadership needs.

## Measuring the Effectiveness of Rest Strategies

**Activity:**

- Develop metrics to assess the effectiveness of your rest strategies. Consider factors like energy levels, productivity, and stress reduction. Track these metrics over a set period.

**Reflection Question:**

- What metrics best reflect the impact of your rest strategies on your leadership performance and well-being? How do these metrics inform your adjustments?

**Tip:**

- Regularly measuring these metrics provides insights into how well your rest strategies support your leadership effectiveness and personal health.

# Evaluating the Impact on Leadership Performance

**Activity:**

- Analyze your performance data before and after implementing rest strategies. Evaluate changes in your decision-making, focus, and overall productivity.

**Reflection Question:**

- How has the integration of strategic rest affected your leadership performance? What specific improvements or challenges have you observed?

**Tip:**

- Assessing performance impact helps you understand the benefits of rest strategies and identify areas for further enhancement.

# Assessing Team Feedback on Leadership Rest

**Activity:**

- Collect feedback from team members on how your rest practices influence your leadership. Use surveys or informal discussions to gauge their perspectives.

**Reflection Question:**

- How do team members perceive the impact of your rest practices on your leadership? What insights can you gather from their feedback?

**Tip:**

- Team feedback provides an external perspective on how your rest practices affect team dynamics and overall effectiveness.

# Analyzing the Balance Between Work and Rest

**Activity:**

- Create a balance chart that maps out your work activities and rest periods. Assess whether your current balance effectively supports your leadership responsibilities and well-being.

**Reflection Question:**

- How does the balance between work and rest in your schedule impact your leadership effectiveness and personal health? What adjustments are needed?

**Tip:**

- Maintaining a proper balance is crucial for sustaining productivity and avoiding burnout. Adjust your schedule as needed to achieve this balance.

# Reviewing Rest Goals and Achievements

**Activity:**

- Review your rest goals and assess whether you have met them. Reflect on how achieving these goals has impacted your leadership performance and personal well-being.

**Reflection Question:**

- What progress have you made toward your rest goals? How has meeting or not meeting these goals influenced your leadership effectiveness?

**Tip:**

- Regular review of rest goals helps ensure that you stay focused on achieving the right balance between work and recovery.

# Identifying Challenges in Rest Practices

**Activity:**

- Document any challenges or barriers you've encountered in maintaining effective rest practices. Analyze their impact on your leadership and develop strategies to address them.

**Reflection Question:**

- What challenges have you faced in prioritizing rest, and how have they affected your leadership? What solutions can you implement to overcome these barriers?

**Tip:**

- Identifying and addressing challenges helps you refine your rest practices and maintain consistent leadership effectiveness.

# Evaluating Long-Term Rest Strategies

**Activity:**

- Reflect on how your rest strategies have evolved over time. Assess their long-term impact on your leadership performance and overall well-being.

**Reflection Question:**

- How have your rest strategies adapted to your changing leadership needs over time? What long-term effects have you observed?

**Tip:**

- Long-term evaluation helps you adapt and optimize your rest strategies to align with evolving leadership demands and personal growth.

# Creating an Improvement Plan

**Activity:**

- Develop an action plan to improve your rest practices based on your assessment findings. Include specific actions, timelines, and methods for tracking progress.

**Reflection Question:**

- What specific improvements can you make to your rest practices based on your assessment? How will you implement and measure these changes?

**Tip:**

- An improvement plan ensures that you systematically enhance your rest practices, leading to better leadership outcomes and personal well-being.

# Reflecting on the Integration of Rest and Leadership

**Activity:**

- Reflect on how effectively you have integrated strategic rest into your leadership approach. Consider how well your rest practices support your overall leadership goals.

**Reflection Question:**

- How well have you integrated strategic rest into your leadership role? What further steps can you take to enhance this integration?

**Tip:**

- Reflecting on the integration of rest into your leadership role helps you ensure that rest is a consistent and effective component of your leadership strategy.

# PRIORITIZE *Your Rest*

## Introduction to Prioritizing Strategic Rest

**Overview:** Strategic rest is a fundamental aspect of effective leadership. Prioritizing rest involves deliberate planning to ensure that recovery and relaxation are integral parts of your leadership strategy. This section introduces how to prioritize rest within your leadership responsibilities.

**Reflection Question:**
- How can prioritizing strategic rest enhance your effectiveness as a leader and improve your overall well-being?

**Tip:**
- Effective leadership requires balancing work and rest. Integrating strategic rest into your priorities can lead to improved performance and reduced burnout.

# Identifying Priorities for Rest

**Activity:**

- List your key leadership responsibilities and personal well-being goals. Identify which aspects of your role and life require prioritizing rest.

**Reflection Question:**

- Which areas of your leadership and personal life most need a strategic focus on rest? How do these areas impact your overall performance and health?

**Tip:**

- Prioritizing rest means recognizing its importance in both your professional responsibilities and personal well-being.

# Scheduling Rest Within Your Leadership Plan

**Activity:**

- Create a detailed schedule that includes both your work commitments and designated rest periods. Ensure that rest is not an afterthought but a planned part of your routine.

**Reflection Question:**

- How does your schedule currently incorporate rest? What changes can you make to ensure that rest periods are effectively prioritized?

**Tip:**

- Incorporate rest into your daily and weekly schedules to maintain a balanced approach to work and recovery.

# Balancing High-Priority Tasks and Rest

**Activity:**

- Use a priority matrix (e.g., the Eisenhower Matrix) to categorize your tasks by urgency and importance. Identify where rest fits into this matrix and adjust your priorities accordingly.

**Reflection Question:**

- How can balancing high-priority tasks with rest improve your productivity and leadership effectiveness? What adjustments do you need to make?

**Tip:**

- Strategic prioritization helps you manage high-priority tasks while ensuring adequate rest is a central part of your schedule.

# Setting Rest Goals

**Activity:**

- Define specific rest goals, such as daily relaxation periods, weekly breaks, and regular vacations. Develop a plan to achieve these goals and integrate them into your leadership strategy.

**Reflection Question:**

- What specific goals can you set to prioritize rest effectively? How will achieving these goals contribute to your leadership success?

**Tip:**

- Setting clear rest goals helps you stay focused on maintaining a balance between work and recovery.

# Evaluating the Impact of Prioritized Rest

**Activity:**

- Track your leadership performance and personal well-being before and after implementing strategic rest priorities. Use metrics such as energy levels, stress reduction, and task efficiency.

**Reflection Question:**

- What impact have prioritized rest periods had on your leadership performance and personal well-being? What changes have you noticed?

**Tip:**

- Regular evaluation of the impact of prioritized rest helps you understand its benefits and make necessary adjustments.

# Adjusting Priorities Based on Rest Needs

**Activity:**

- Assess your current priorities and determine if adjustments are needed to better accommodate rest. Reallocate tasks or responsibilities as necessary to ensure adequate recovery.

**Reflection Question:**

- How do your current priorities support or hinder your need for rest? What changes can you make to better align your priorities with rest needs?

**Tip:**

- Adjusting priorities to include sufficient rest ensures you maintain productivity while avoiding burnout.

# Communicating Priorities to Your Team

**Activity:**

- Develop a communication plan to share your prioritization of rest with your team. Explain how this approach benefits both your leadership and the team's overall performance.

**Reflection Question:**

- How can communicating your focus on rest to your team enhance their understanding and support of your leadership strategy?

**Tip:**

- Open communication about the importance of rest fosters a supportive environment and encourages team members to also prioritize their well-being.

# Reflecting on Long-Term Prioritization

**Activity:**

- Reflect on how your approach to prioritizing rest has evolved over time. Consider the long-term effects of these priorities on your leadership and personal life.

**Reflection Question:**

- How have your long-term priorities regarding rest influenced your leadership journey? What have you learned about balancing work and recovery?

**Tip:**

- Long-term reflection helps you refine your approach to prioritizing rest and ensures it aligns with your evolving leadership goals.

## Creating a Strategic Rest Action Plan

**Activity:**

- Develop a comprehensive action plan to integrate strategic rest into your leadership priorities. Include specific actions, deadlines, and accountability measures.

**Reflection Question:**

- What specific steps will you take to ensure that rest is effectively prioritized in your leadership role? How will you track and measure your success?

**Tip:**

- An actionable plan with clear steps and deadlines helps you implement strategic rest consistently and effectively.

# Appendix C

# 21-Day Strategic Rest Action Plan Using the N.A.P. Framework

**Objective:** To integrate strategic rest into your leadership practice over 21 days, enhancing leadership effectiveness, personal well-being, and overall performance.

Use this 21-day plan to systematically integrate strategic rest into your leadership role. By nurturing effective rest practices, assessing their impact, and prioritizing rest in your schedule, you will enhance both your leadership effectiveness and personal well-being. Regularly review and adjust your plan to maintain a balanced and effective approach to leadership.

# Days 1-7: Nurture - Cultivating Personal Rest Practices

**Goal:** Develop and maintain personal habits and routines that support effective rest and recovery, enhancing leadership effectiveness.

# Day 1: Establish Rest Routines

- **Action:** Create daily and weekly routines specifically designed to include rest and relaxation periods.
- **Reflection Question:** How can establishing consistent rest routines improve your leadership effectiveness?
- **Your Plan:**

_____

_____

_____

_____

_____

_____

_____

_____

_____

_____

_____

_____

_____

_____

_____

_____

_____

_____

_____

_____

_____

# Day 2: Design a Supportive Environment

- **Action:** Arrange your workspace and home environment to facilitate relaxation and minimize stressors.
- **Reflection Question:** What environmental changes can enhance your ability to rest and recharge?
- **Your Plan:**

_____

_____

_____

_____

_____

_____

_____

_____

_____

_____

_____

_____

_____

_____

_____

_____

_____

_____

_____

_____

# Day 3: Set Professional and Personal Boundaries

- **Action:** Define clear boundaries between work and personal time to protect your rest and prevent burnout.
- **Reflection Question:** How does establishing boundaries between work and personal life impact your leadership performance?
- **Your Plan:**

_____

_____

_____

_____

_____

_____

_____

_____

_____

_____

_____

_____

_____

_____

_____

_____

_____

_____

_____

# Day 4: Schedule Regular Breaks

- **Action:** Integrate short, frequent breaks into your workday to refresh your mind and sustain productivity.
- **Reflection Question:** How does taking regular breaks affect your focus and decision-making in leadership roles?
- **Your Plan:**

---
---
---
---
---
---
---
---
---
---
---
---
---
---
---
---
---
---
---
---
---

# Day 5: Incorporate Mindfulness Practices

- **Action:** Integrate mindfulness techniques or meditation into your daily routine to reduce stress and enhance clarity.
- **Reflection Question:** How can mindfulness practices improve your leadership presence and effectiveness?
- **Your Plan:**

# Day 6: Develop a Consistent Sleep Schedule

- **Action:** Create and stick to a consistent sleep schedule to boost energy levels and cognitive function.
- **Reflection Question:** How does a regular sleep schedule impact your ability to lead effectively and make sound decisions?
- **Your Plan:**

_____

_____

_____

_____

_____

_____

_____

_____

_____

_____

_____

_____

_____

_____

_____

_____

_____

_____

_____

_____

_____

# Day 7: Reflect on Your Rest Practices

- **Action:** Review the effectiveness of your rest practices over the past week and make adjustments as needed.
- **Reflection Question:** What adjustments to your rest practices have shown the most significant impact on your leadership effectiveness?
- **Your Plan:**

_____

_____

_____

_____

_____

_____

_____

_____

_____

_____

_____

_____

_____

_____

_____

_____

_____

_____

_____

_____

_____

_____

# Days 8-14: Assess - Evaluating the Impact of Rest Practices

**Goal:** Evaluate the effectiveness of your rest practices in enhancing leadership effectiveness and adjust as needed.

# Day 8: Track Well-Being and Leadership Performance

- **Action:** Use self-assessment tools to monitor your energy levels, stress, and leadership performance.
- **Reflection Question:** What trends do you notice in your well-being and leadership performance related to your rest practices?
- **Your Plan:**

_____
_____
_____
_____
_____
_____
_____
_____
_____
_____
_____
_____
_____
_____
_____
_____
_____
_____
_____
_____

# Day 9: Review Rest Utilization

- **Action:** Reflect on how frequently and effectively you have been utilizing rest practices and their impact on leadership.
- **Reflection Question:** How effectively are you incorporating rest into your daily leadership activities?
- **Your Plan:**

_____

_____

_____

_____

_____

_____

_____

_____

_____

_____

_____

_____

_____

_____

_____

_____

_____

_____

_____

_____

# Day 10: Seek Feedback on Leadership and Rest

- **Action:** Gather feedback from mentors or peers on how your rest practices have influenced your leadership.
- **Reflection Question:** What feedback have you received regarding the impact of your rest practices on your leadership?
- **Your Plan:**

_____

_____

_____

_____

_____

_____

_____

_____

_____

_____

_____

_____

_____

_____

_____

_____

_____

_____

_____

_____

# Day 11: Analyze Energy and Stress Levels

- **Action:** Evaluate fluctuations in your energy and stress levels and their impact on leadership tasks.
- **Reflection Question:** How do changes in your energy and stress levels affect your leadership effectiveness?
- **Your Plan:**

_____

_____

_____

_____

_____

_____

_____

_____

_____

_____

_____

_____

_____

_____

_____

_____

_____

_____

_____

_____

_____

_____

# Day 12: Assess Stress Management Strategies

- **Action:** Review the effectiveness of your stress management strategies in relation to your rest practices.
- **Reflection Question:** How well are your stress management strategies working to support your leadership role?
- **Your Plan:**

_____

_____

_____

_____

_____

_____

_____

_____

_____

_____

_____

_____

_____

_____

_____

_____

_____

_____

_____

_____

# Day 13: Evaluate Productivity and Leadership Impact

- **Action:** Assess how your rest practices influence productivity and leadership outcomes.
- **Reflection Question:** How has your productivity and ability to lead been impacted by your rest practices?
- **Your Plan:**

_____

_____

_____

_____

_____

_____

_____

_____

_____

_____

_____

_____

_____

_____

_____

_____

_____

_____

_____

_____

_____

# Day 14: Refine Rest Practices Based on Assessments

- **Action:** Make necessary adjustments to your rest practices based on your assessment findings.
- **Reflection Question:** What specific changes will you implement to enhance the effectiveness of your rest practices in your leadership role?
- **Your Plan:**

_____

_____

_____

_____

_____

_____

_____

_____

_____

_____

_____

_____

_____

_____

_____

_____

_____

_____

_____

_____

_____

## Days 15-21: Prioritize - Integrating Rest into Your Leadership Schedule

**Goal:** Ensure that strategic rest is a fundamental part of your daily and weekly schedule, balancing it with leadership responsibilities.

# Day 15: Schedule Dedicated Rest Periods

- **Action:** Allocate specific times in your calendar for rest and personal activities, ensuring they are protected from work interruptions.
- **Reflection Question:** How does scheduling dedicated rest periods affect your leadership efficiency and effectiveness?
- **Your Plan:**

_____

_____

_____

_____

_____

_____

_____

_____

_____

_____

_____

_____

_____

_____

_____

_____

_____

_____

_____

_____

_____

# Day 16: Balance Leadership Tasks and Rest

- **Action:** Use tools like time-blocking or priority matrices to ensure a balanced approach between leadership tasks and rest.
- **Reflection Question:** How do you manage the balance between your leadership responsibilities and rest periods?
- **Your Plan:**

---
---
---
---
---
---
---
---
---
---
---
---
---
---
---
---
---
---
---
---
---
---
---
---
---
---

# Day 17: Set Clear Rest Goals

- **Action:** Define and document specific goals for the amount of rest you aim to achieve each week.
- **Reflection Question:** What are your rest goals, and how do they align with your leadership priorities?
- **Your Plan:**

_____

_____

_____

_____

_____

_____

_____

_____

_____

_____

_____

_____

_____

_____

_____

_____

_____

_____

_____

_____

_____

_____

_____

_____

## Day 18: Integrate Rest into Leadership Activities

- **Action:** Find ways to incorporate rest and recovery strategies into your leadership tasks and meetings.
- **Reflection Question:** How can you incorporate rest practices into your leadership activities to enhance effectiveness?
- **Your Plan:**

_____
_____
_____
_____
_____
_____
_____
_____
_____
_____
_____
_____
_____
_____
_____
_____
_____
_____
_____
_____
_____

# Day 19: Monitor and Adjust Rest and Productivity Balance

- **Action:** Track how well you are balancing rest with productivity and adjust your schedule as needed.
- **Reflection Question:** How does the balance between rest and productivity impact your leadership performance?
- **Your Plan:**

_____

_____

_____

_____

_____

_____

_____

_____

_____

_____

_____

_____

_____

_____

_____

_____

_____

_____

_____

# Day 20: Evaluate and Adapt Your Schedule

- **Action:** Review and adjust your schedule based on your experiences with integrating rest and balancing responsibilities.

- **Reflection Question:** What adjustments will improve the integration of rest into your leadership schedule?

- **Your Plan:**

_____

_____

_____

_____

_____

_____

_____

_____

_____

_____

_____

_____

_____

_____

_____

_____

_____

_____

_____

_____

_____

_____

# Day 21: Reflect and Plan for Sustained Integration

- **Action:** Reflect on the past 21 days and plan how to continue integrating strategic rest into your leadership practice long term.
- **Reflection Question:** How will you sustain the integration of strategic rest into your ongoing leadership practice?
- **Your Plan:**

_____

_____

_____

_____

_____

_____

_____

_____

_____

_____

_____

_____

_____

_____

_____

_____

_____

_____

_____

_____

# Appendix D

# A Guide for Collective Strategic Rest

### 1. Expand Your Team

Think of your team as more than just your immediate colleagues. Include people from different areas—industry peers, mastermind group members, or even folks from other fields who share your values. A diverse support network can give you fresh ideas and broader support, making your journey less lonely.

### 2. Build a Supportive Community

Join or start a mastermind group where people share experiences, offer feedback, and support each other's growth. These groups are great for boosting your rest practices and getting practical advice from others who are on a similar path.

### 3. Share and Encourage Rest Practices

Talk about what's working for you in terms of rest and well-being with your network. When you model good rest practices and encourage others to do the same, you help build a culture that values taking care of ourselves.

### 4. Get and Use Feedback

Check in regularly with your network to see how your rest practices are working. Be open to feedback and ready to tweak your strategies based on what you hear. This helps keep your approach fresh and effective for everyone involved.

### 5. Quarterly Meetups

- **Action:** Set aside time every three months to catch up, share experiences, and reflect on your journey with rest.
- **How:** Structure your meet-ups with focused conversations, reflective exercises, and discussions on themes related to strategic rest. Use this time to recharge and rejuvenate.

### 6. Share and Learn from Each Other

- **Action:** Use your gatherings to tap into the collective wisdom of your group.
- **How:** Choose a theme each quarter (like work-life balance) and discuss your strategies and experiences related to that theme. This sharing can offer new insights and support.

### 7. Have Honest Conversations

- **Action:** Be open about the challenges and successes of integrating rest into your leadership.
- **How:** Facilitate discussions that encourage transparency and problem-solving. Use reflective activities to dig deeper and personalize your approach to rest.

### 8. Plan and Adjust

- **Action:** Create practical strategies for better rest and make sure they work for you.

- **How:** Develop action plans based on your discussions, set specific rest goals, and have follow-up chats to review progress and make adjustments.

## 9. Energize and Reconnect

- **Action:** End each gathering on a high note, feeling refreshed and reconnected with your goals.
- **How:** Wrap up with a reflective activity to reinforce what you've learned and celebrate your achievements.

### Invitation to connect - Collectively!

Our quarterly approach to collective strategic rest has been transformative for our leadership journey. The insights gained from our regular reflections and discussions have been crucial in shaping the practices outlined in this book. By sharing our experiences, we hope to inspire you to embrace strategic rest in your own leadership journey.

# Appendix E

# Be-Do-Have: Concept for Strategic Rest in Leadership

**Activity: Becoming a Leader Who Embodies Strategic Rest**

## 1. Define the Leader You Need to Become (Be):

- **Activity:** Write a brief description of the type of leader you aspire to be, focusing on qualities related to strategic rest. Consider traits such as being mindful, balanced, and proactive in managing rest.
- **Example:** "I want to be a leader who is fully present, balances work with personal time, and models healthy rest practices for my team."

## 2. Identify the Actions You Need to Take (Do):

- **Activity:** List specific actions that align with the leader you want to become. These might include setting boundaries, scheduling regular breaks, or practicing mindfulness.
- **Example:** "Schedule daily 10-minute mindfulness breaks, set clear work boundaries, and plan regular team wellness activities."

## 3. Envision What You Will Achieve (Have):

- **Activity:** Visualize and describe the outcomes of embodying strategic rest. Think about how these changes will impact your leadership effectiveness and overall well-being.

- **Example:** "By embodying strategic rest, I will lead a more engaged and motivated team, experience reduced stress, and achieve greater work-life balance."

**Reflection Question:** How do the qualities and actions you've identified support the integration of strategic rest into your leadership style, and how will they impact your effectiveness and well-being?

**Tip:** Regularly revisit and update your Be-Do-Have plan to ensure alignment with your evolving goals and to reinforce the practices that help you become the leader you aspire to be.

# NOTES

Chapter 2
1. McPherson, M., Smith-Lovin, L., & Cook, J. M. (2001). Birds of a Feather: Homophily in Social Networks. Annual Review of Sociology, 27, 415–444. http://www.jstor.org/stable/2678628
2. Dalton-Smith, S. (2017). Sacred Rest: Recover Your Life, Renew Your Energy, Restore Your Sanity.
3. Scudder, T. (n.d.). *Core strengths SDI 2.0 methodology and meaning.* CoreStrengths. https://www.corestrengths.com/sdi-2-0-methodology-and-meaning/

Chapter 3
1. Murphy, M. (2010). *Hard goals: The secret to getting from where you are to where you want to be.* McGraw Hill.
2. SMART Goals, acronym for Smart, Measurable, Actionable, Realistic, Time-Bound
3. HARD goals, acronym for Heartfelt, Animated, Required, Difficult
4. Covey, S. R. (1989). *The seven habits of highly effective people: restoring the character ethic.* New York, Simon and Schuster.

Chapter 6
1. Neese, A. (2023). *Permission to rest: Revolutionary practices for healing, empowerment, and collective care.* Ten Speed Press.

# ABOUT THE AUTHORS

**Dr. Kellie Dixon** is the author of Recharge: Self-Awareness Approach to Goal Achievement and Reclaiming Our Affirmations, higher education professional, minority owner of the Carolina Cobras (professional arena football team), and CEO/Founder of Clear Pathway Consulting Services LLC. With a doctorate degree in Organizational Leadership and a master's in Counseling, she has built a career in leadership development, where she has developed a deep expertise in self-awareness. Dr. Dixon combines this professional background with a keen interest in the role of strategic rest in fostering creativity and productivity. She is known for disrupting narratives that no longer serve you (us). Outside of writing, Dr. Dixon enjoys strategically resting with her yorkie poo, Kofi, and resides in North Carolina. Learn more about Dr. Dixon at www.clearpathwaycs.com

**Dr. Erin Wilson**, founder and principal consultant of Design Ideal Consulting, is passionate about helping individuals and teams reach their full potential by leveraging relationship intelligence. With more than a decade of experience in leadership, learning and development, and community engagement, Erin has facilitated team-building and staff retreat sessions for organizations and universities across the country. She holds a doctorate in Organizational Leadership along with a master's in Human Development and Leadership. Inspired by the transformative power of strategic rest in her life, Dr. Wilson partnered with Dr. Kellie Dixon to write this book to show leaders how intentional rest can unlock clarity, resilience, and creativity. When she's not working, she enjoys traveling with her husband, Fredarick, and spending time with her beloved pitty, Harley Quinn. Learn more about Dr. Wilson at www.designidealconsulting.com